CONTENTS

THE ART OF VIDEO GAME TESTING: A COMPREHENSIVE GUIDE

DISCLAIMER

Disclaimer: The information contained in this book is for educational and entertainment purposes only. The author and publisher of this book are not responsible for any misuse or misinterpretation of the information provided, nor do they guarantee the accuracy, completeness, or timeliness of the information. The techniques, strategies, and opinions presented in this book are solely those of the author and should not be construed as professional advice. Readers should consult with a qualified expert before making any decisions or taking any actions based on the information presented in this book. The author and publisher disclaim any liability for any damages or losses that may result from the use of the information presented in this book.

The trademarks, logos, and intellectual property (IP) mentioned in this book are the property of their respective owners. The use of such trademarks and logos is for informational purposes only and does not constitute an endorsement, sponsorship, or affiliation by the owner of the trademark or logo. Any unauthorized use of these trademarks, logos, or IP is strictly prohibited. The author and publisher of this book make no claims or representations as to the ownership of any trademark or IP mentioned in this book. The author and publisher also make no warranties or guarantees, express or implied, regarding the accuracy, completeness, or reliability of the information presented in this book. Readers should seek legal counsel before taking any action based on the information presented in this book. The author and publisher disclaim any liability for any damages or losses that may result from the use of the information presented in this book.

Email Enquiries: **henryhanley@hotmail.co.uk**

CHAPTER 1 - WHY VIDEO GAME TESTING IS SUPER IMPORTANT?

Do you love playing video games? Who Doesn't? Well, you can thank video game testers for making sure the games you play are free from bugs and glitches!

Video game testing is an essential component of the development process that guarantees the game works correctly, without any technical issues. So, the next time you play your favourite game, take a moment to acknowledge the hard work of video game testers who have contributed to making your gaming experience enjoyable!

You know yourself, if a game is full of bugs and runs with dodgy frame rates for example, you are going to get frustrated with it and more than likely, want your money back. You will also tell friends and other gamers in any gaming communities or circles you are a part of that the game is terrible and would not recommend it to others. This will of course reduce sales for the game.

This is why video game testers are extremely important in checking and testing any code, design, game mechanic or logic changes made to the game and make sure that it doesn't break anything else that was working previously before in the game.

Let's briefly explore why video game testing is so important and the ways it can make or break a game.

Quality Assurance

Have you ever played a game and found a glitch or bug that ruined your experience? We have all been there right? Even if the game was working perfectly before and you have had to download the latest update or patch, this can sometimes cause mayhem with features that worked previously before this patch was downloaded and installed.

This, of course, is not what the developers of the game intended. Developers want to fix any previous bugs in the game and enhance it, rather than break it, ensuring games run more smoothly and bug free than it did before after every update.

Video game testing helps avoid a mess like that occurring in the first place. By testing the game before release, testers can identify and report any issues, which are then fixed by the developers before the game hits the shelves in stores or arrives digitally on our consoles, or PC's, gaming dashboards.

This makes sure the final game is free from major technical issues and works the way it's designed to from the start. Without testing, games could be released with serious issues that impact the player's experience, leading to bad reviews, fewer sales and a damaged reputation for the game publisher or developer.

To ensure that a product or service meets specific quality standards and requirements before it is deemed ready for release, Quality Assurance (QA) is the process used. It is a collection of tasks and actions that aim to guarantee a consistent and dependable product or service that satisfies the demands and expectations of consumers.

The objective of quality assurance is to eradicate errors and faults before delivering a product or service to the ultimate customer or consumer. Various methods and processes, such as inspections, testing, and documentation, can be used to achieve this.

QA processes typically include planning, designing, and performing tests to discover and resolve problems that emerge during the testing stages before delivering the product or service to the customer. The exact steps of these tests may differ across industries, as each industry has its own unique requirements.

Implementing efficient QA procedures is a critical aspect of any industry or business that produces goods or services, as it aids in maintaining the company's reputation and ensuring customer satisfaction and loyalty. By adopting effective QA protocols, businesses can decrease expenses, increase efficiency, and boost profitability.

User Experience

Video game testing not only ensures that the game functions as intended but also contributes to improving the user experience as a whole. Testers can report issues like unintuitive controls, confounding User Interfaces or unfortunate game equilibrium which may not be apparent to the developers at the coding stages. The game's mechanics, tutorial or user interface can then be altered by developers in order to addresses these issues before they get too deep into developing the game.

The further development goes along with these problems within the game, the harder it can be to fix them at a later stage, if at all. Video game testing can assist in the development of games that are enjoyable and engaging for players by concentrating on the user experience and making it the best it can be.

The term "User Experience" (UX) refers to a user's overall satisfaction and experience when utilizing a system, product, or service. It includes usability, accessibility, design and functionality, as well as all aspects of the user's interaction.

Product and system design that creates a positive user experience is known as UX design. This requires designing products that are intuitive, user-friendly and pleasing to the eye, while also comprehending the user's requirements and objectives.

To create products that satisfy the requirements of customers, user experience (UX) designers employ a variety of methods to come up with the best way for a user to interact with their product, including user research, usability testing and prototyping.

The objective of UX configuration is to make items and frameworks that are practical and proficient, yet in addition, agreeable and fulfilling to utilize. Companies can increase user engagement, customer loyalty and overall customer satisfaction by providing a positive user experience.

In conclusion, user experience (UX) design is an essential component of product and service design. It entails comprehending the requirements and objectives of the user and creating systems and products that satisfy their needs accordingly.

Reputation

The success of a game often depends on its reputation. By ensuring that the game is free of bugs and glitches and provides players with an enjoyable experience, video game testing contributes to the development of that reputation. Developers can establish a positive reputation by releasing a high-quality game, which will result in increased sales, devoted fans, and continued success.

The quality of the game itself, the marketing and promotion of the game, and the opinions and reviews of players and critics all have an impact on a game's reputation. In the event that a game has a positive standing, it is bound to be generally welcomed by players and produce positive verbal exchange buzz, which can prompt expanded deals and income. On the other hand, if a game has a bad reputation, it may have trouble attracting players and selling products.

The reputation of a game can also be affected by its success. On the off chance that a game is fruitful, it could be seen as a great and very much planned item, which can support its standing and lead to positive surveys and player input. On the other hand, if a game doesn't do well, people might think it's a lower-quality product. This can hurt the game's reputation and get bad reviews and feedback from players.

A game's reputation can be seriously damaged by bugs, as can the game's overall success and profitability. Bugs can go from minor issues, for example, visual errors or little mistakes in ongoing interaction, to additional difficult issues, for example, crashes, game-breaking bugs, or takes advantage of that permit players to cheat or acquire an unreasonable benefit.

Bugs can have a significant impact on a game's reputation in a number of ways, one of which is by lowering the game's overall quality and polish. Bugs can detract from the overall player experience and give a game the impression of not being finished or polished. Players might become baffled or irritated by bugs, and might be more averse to prescribe the game to other people or buy future games from a similar engineer.

A game's reputation can also be harmed by bugs, which can result in negative press and reviews. The game may receive negative reviews from critics and players, highlighting bugs and other issues. This can hurt the developer's or publisher's reputation and result in lower revenue and sales.

Before the game is released, developers need to make an investment in thorough testing and quality assurance procedures to find and fix bugs. They should also disclose any known issues with the game and regularly release patches and updates to fix them. Developers have the ability to maintain a positive reputation and cultivate a loyal player base if they place a high value on quality and address bugs quickly and effectively.

In a nutshell, a game's success and its reputation are inextricably linked. A game's success can be aided by a positive reputation, while its failure can hurt its chances. Publishers and developers must carefully consider how to manage a game's reputation and work to develop high-quality games that attract players and generate positive buzz.

Cost Savings

Although video game testing can be costly initially, it has the potential to ultimately save money. Developers can avoid spending a lot of money on patches and fixes after the game is released by finding and fixing problems during testing. A high-quality game also results in fewer returns, refunds, and negative reviews, saving money in the long run. Developers can ensure their game's success and profitability by investing in testing.

Reducing the cost of fixing bugs and other issues after the game has been released is one of the main ways that game testing can save money. When a game is released with bugs or other issues, developers may need to spend a lot of time and money to find and fix those problems, such as patching the game and responding to complaints from customers. This procedure can be costly, time-consuming, and damaging to both the game and its creator.

By conducting thorough game testing prior to its release, developers can proactively detect and resolve potential problems in the early stages of development. This preemptive approach helps prevent issues from escalating into larger and more expensive complications. Investing in comprehensive game testing not only reduces the overall cost of issue resolution but also ensures that the game is delivered with a high level of quality and polish.

Reducing the likelihood of costly delays or cancellations is another way that game testing can save money in the long run. If a game is released with a lot of bugs or issues, players may not like it, and sales or revenue goals may be hard to reach. This may result in the cancellation of future projects as well as delays in the development of future games.

Developers can ensure that their games are well-received by

players and reduce the risk of these issues by investing in thorough game testing. In the long run, this can assist in maintaining the developer's reputation, fostering customer loyalty, and ultimately increasing revenue.

In synopsis, while game testing can be costly, it can set aside cash over the long haul by lessening the expense of fixing bugs and different issues after the game has been delivered, as well as decreasing the gamble of exorbitant postponements or scratch-offs. Developers can build a loyal player base, increase revenue over time, and ensure that their games are released with a high level of quality and polish by investing in thorough game testing.

Testing video games is essential for making high-quality games that players will enjoy playing. Video game testing is crucial to a game's success because it focuses on quality assurance, user experience, reputation, and cost savings. Video game developers who make an investment in testing can produce games that are not only enjoyable to play but also profitable over time. Therefore, the next time you play a game without any glitches, keep in mind to express gratitude to the testers who made it possible!

The Role of a Video Game Tester

With the ongoing expansion of the computer game industry, there is a parallel increase in the need for proficient and seasoned video game testers. These testers play a vital role in guaranteeing the readiness and refinement of games by diligently uncovering and documenting gameplay issues, bugs, and errors for the development team to address. In this chapter, we delve into the essential skills and qualifications required for individuals aspiring to thrive as video game testers.

Before games can be released to the public, they need to undergo thorough testing by video game testers. This typically involves playing the game multiple times, looking for glitches and bugs, and providing feedback on the overall user experience, level design, and gameplay mechanics. Video game testers are essential for maintaining the quality of games by identifying problems and suggesting improvements.

A prosperous career in video game testing necessitates a range of crucial abilities and qualifications. These encompass a keen eye for detail, exceptional communication skills, and a profound comprehension of the video game industry. Video game testers must possess the capability to promptly and clearly communicate any identified issues to the development team, regardless of their perceived significance. Additionally, they should excel in collaborating with other developers, offering valuable feedback on gameplay mechanics and level design in a cohesive manner.

Furthermore, video game testers must possess a comprehensive knowledge of the video game industry, keeping up-to-date with the latest trends and advancements and having a profound understanding of different game genres and types. This allows them to provide insightful feedback on gameplay mechanics and user experience.

In addition to these skills, video game testers must have a genuine passion for video games, as testing them can be a challenging and demanding job. Testers must be able to concentrate for long periods of time while remaining enthusiastic and willing to play games and find issues.

What Skills Do Games Companies Look For In A Games Tester?

Game testers are typically hired by game developers who are looking for a combination of personal qualities and technical skills. Depending on the role and the needs of the development team, different skills and characteristics may be valued more than others, but some common ones are:

Technical expertise: In addition to having a working knowledge of programming languages, testing suites, and software development kits (SDKs), a games tester should have a solid understanding of game development and testing procedures. They should have worked with a variety of game engines and platforms and be familiar with bug reporting and tracking systems.

Attention to particulars: Testers should have a sharp eye for detail and have the ability to detect even the smallest bugs or issues in a game. In order for developers to effectively comprehend and address issues, they ought to be able to consistently replicate the issue and clearly document steps on how to reproduce the issue.

Skills for communicating: To effectively communicate with other members of the development team, games testers should have strong verbal and written communication skills. They ought to have the option to give clear and brief criticism on issues, and ought to have the option to work cooperatively with developers to address them.

Skills for solving problems: Testers should be able to work games development team to find effective solutions to complex issues. They ought to be able to think creatively and devise novel strategies for evaluating the game and locating issues.

Love of video games: Testers often value having a passion for video games. They ought to be enthusiastic about playing games and well-versed in the elements that make games enjoyable and engaging for players.

Teamwork: Testers should be able to work well in a group setting and with other testers, developers, and stakeholders to find and fix problems in the game together.

Using time productively: To ensure that a game is thoroughly tested before it is released, game testers should be able to effectively manage their time and work effectively to meet deadlines.

In conclusion, when hiring games testers, game developers will look for a combination of personal qualities and technical skills, such as attention to detail, communication skills, problem-solving abilities, a passion for games, teamwork, and time management.

Developers can guarantee that their games are thoroughly tested and polished before they are made available to the general public by finding and hiring testers who possess these characteristics.

What Qualifications Do I Need?

You don't necessarily need a specific degree qualification to get started in this field. While having a degree or diploma in computer science, software engineering, or a related field can certainly be helpful in developing the technical skills and knowledge required for the job, many video game companies also value relevant experience and a passion for gaming.

The Different Types of Testing

As a video game tester, you get to do all sorts of testing to ensure that a game is perfect for release. There are different types of testing, including:

Testing of Functions: This type of testing focuses on making sure that the game mechanics work correctly. You check things like the physics, animations, and controls to ensure they're functioning as intended.

Tests of Compatibility: The game undergoes compatibility testing to ensure that it works correctly on different platforms, such as PCs, consoles, and mobile devices. The game is tested in various hardware and software configurations to find compatibility issues.

Evaluation of Performance: Performance testing helps find any issues with the game's performance, such as lag or drops in frame rate. You test the game under various conditions, such as different network conditions, system loads, and graphics settings.

Relapse Testing: This type of testing makes sure that any issues that were recently fixed have not resurfaced or caused new problems.

Testing for Localization: This testing ensures that the game has been appropriately translated and localized for different languages and regions. You play the game in various languages to check for any cultural or translation errors.

Testing of User Acceptance: A group of players test a game's user acceptance to make sure it meets their expectations and provides an enjoyable gaming experience.

By doing these different types of testing, video game testers make sure that a game is of the highest quality and ready for public release.

CHAPTER 2 - THE FUNDAMENTALS OF VIDEO GAME TESTING

Video game testing is an essential part of the game development process, ensuring that games are of high quality and ready for release to the public. In this chapter, we will explore the fundamentals of video game testing, including the testing process, the role of a tester, and the different techniques used in game testing.

Here is a brief outline and high level over view of the various testing stages that a video game goes through from start to finish:

Planning: The game development team creates a plan for testing the game, including which features and components will be tested, how they will be tested, and what the test criteria will be.

Game development teams create a testing plan for video game testers during the planning stage by first defining the testing objectives. They determine what aspects of the game need to be tested, such as gameplay mechanics, user interface, graphics, and sound. They then identify the testing methods and tools that will be used to ensure that the game meets the desired quality standards.

The team also devises the testing schedule and determines the optimal number of testers required to fulfil all testing obligations. They establish an effective communication strategy to facilitate timely feedback from testers regarding any identified issues during the testing phase. Moreover, the team may implement a bug tracking system to monitor and prioritize the reported issues.

In essence, the objective is to formulate a comprehensive testing plan that encompasses all facets of the game, guaranteeing that the end product achieves superior quality and fulfils players' expectations.

Pre-Alpha Testing: The game is tested in its very early stages, focusing mainly on basic functionality, core mechanics, and level design.

When a video game is in the pre-alpha testing stage, game testers will typically focus on testing the core functionality of the game. This includes checking that the basic mechanics are working as intended, such as movement and combat systems. Testers will also look for any major bugs or glitches that could affect the overall experience of the game.

In addition to these technical aspects, testers may also provide feedback on the game's aesthetics and user interface. The goal of pre-alpha testing is to identify any major issues early on in the development process so they can be addressed before the game moves into later stages of development.

Alpha Testing: This is the first major testing phase, where the game is feature-complete and mostly stable. Alpha testing focuses on testing the game's various systems and mechanics, identifying and reporting bugs, and providing feedback to improve the overall experience.

Game Testers test the various game mechanics, gameplay features, and levels to ensure they are functioning as intended. Testers may also provide feedback on the game's difficulty level, pacing, and overall user experience. Additionally, they may test the game's performance under various conditions and provide recommendations for improvements.

Overall, the goal of alpha testing is to identify and address any major issues or flaws in the game before it moves on to the beta testing stage.

Beta Testing: This stage involves testing the game on a larger scale, usually with a group of external testers or the public. Beta testing is focused on bug fixing, balancing the game, and collecting feedback from a wider audience.

In the beta stage of video game testing, a collaborative effort takes place involving both video game testers and members of the public who are invited to test the game. Their aim is to diligently examine the game for bugs, glitches, and other potential issues that could impact the overall gameplay experience. The primary objective is to identify and rectify as many issues as possible before the game is officially launched to the public.

Beyond technical concerns, testers also contribute valuable feedback on various aspects, including gameplay mechanics, game balance, and user interface. This feedback plays a crucial role in making necessary adjustments and improvements, ensuring the game is optimized prior to its release.

The feedback from the public users is usually taken into account during the beta testing phase. Game developers often gather feedback from beta testers through various channels such as surveys, forums, and social media. They then analyze the feedback and use it to make improvements to the game before its final release.

This helps ensure that the game meets the expectations of the target audience and provides an enjoyable gaming experience.

Release Candidate: The game is nearly complete and is tested extensively to identify and resolve any remaining issues, such as critical bugs or crashes.

During the release candidate stage of the game testing process, the focus is on making sure the game is as close to perfect as possible before it is released to the public. This phase involves conducting final tests on the game to ensure that all known bugs and issues have been resolved. The game is tested on various platforms to ensure that it functions properly and is stable.

Additionally, the game is reviewed by the development team to make sure that it meets all of the project's requirements and specifications. Once the game is deemed ready, it is released to the public.

Gold Master: The gold master stage signifies the ultimate phase of game development, marking the completion of all testing and approval for public release.

During this stage, the game reaches its finalized form, deemed ready for manufacturing and distribution. Games testers play a crucial role in conducting final checks to ensure the game's stability and the absence of significant bugs or glitches.

The testing team may undertake a final round of thorough testing to confirm the resolution of any previously identified issues and ensure the game aligns with the quality standards established by the development team. Once the testing team grants their approval, the game stands prepared for its public release.

Post-Release Testing: After the game is released, testing continues to identify and resolve any issues that may arise, such as bugs, glitches, and other problems reported by players that may only be noticeable when the game is played by thousands of people at a time, such as low frame rates when an excessive number of players are in a certain area is an example.

In the post-release phase, game testers actively focus on discovering and reporting any overlooked bugs or issues that might have eluded earlier testing stages. They conduct comprehensive testing in diverse scenarios and environments to assess the game's performance and stability. Furthermore, they diligently gather player feedback and closely monitor forums and social media platforms to identify any issues encountered by players.

Using this valuable feedback, testers compile detailed bug reports and collaborate with the development team to prioritize and address these issues through patches and updates. Additionally, they may contribute to devising strategies and plans for future testing initiatives and overall game enhancement.

Understanding the Benefits of Video Game Testing

Video game testing offers several benefits to game developers, including:

Identifying Bugs and Issues: The primary purpose of video game testing is to identify bugs and issues in the game. Through testing, developers can identify and resolve issues before the game is released to the public, resulting in a better gaming experience for players.

Ensuring Quality: Video game testing is essential in ensuring that the game is of high quality and meets the standards expected by players. Testing allows developers to identify areas that require improvement, ensuring that the game is as polished and enjoyable as possible.

Enhancing Gameplay: Testing helps developers identify gameplay issues and improve the game's overall experience. By addressing gameplay issues and making adjustments to the game mechanics, developers can create a game that is more fun and engaging for players.

Increasing Customer Satisfaction: By releasing a high-quality game, developers can increase customer satisfaction and build a positive reputation, resulting in increased sales and success. Players will return to a game series if they know it works well, has no bugs, or very minor ones that do not interrupt the game playing experience, resulting in more sales and copies of the game sold digitally or physically.

The Role of Video Game Testing
in Game Development

Game testing is crucial for game development as it ensures that the game is of high quality and is free from glitches and bugs. This helps to enhance the player's overall gaming experience and ensures that the game is successful.

Game testers assume a vital responsibility in detecting and reporting game issues across different testing phases, enabling developers to rectify them prior to the game's public release. This systematic approach not only saves time and resources for game development companies but also ensures the delivery of a refined and fully functional game to players.

Video game testing plays an integral role in the overall game development process, encompassing several crucial functions. These functions include:

Ensuring the Game is Stable: Testing ensures that the game is stable and does not crash or freeze during gameplay. By identifying and addressing stability issues, developers can create a game that is more reliable and enjoyable for players.

Developers help to ensure a game is stable by fixing bugs and glitches during the development process, implementing code optimization techniques, and performing rigorous testing before releasing the game to the public. They also closely monitor the game after release and release patches or updates to address any issues that arise.

Additionally, developers often collaborate with game testers to receive feedback and identify any areas for improvement. By taking these measures, developers can create a stable and enjoyable gaming experience for players.

Ensuring the Game is Bug-Free: Testing helps identify and eliminate bugs and glitches, resulting in a smoother gameplay experience for players.

It is practically impossible to guarantee that a game is completely bug-free. However, game developers can take measures to reduce the likelihood of bugs appearing, such as conducting thorough testing at each stage of development and fixing any issues that arise promptly.

They can also incorporate automated testing tools to assist in identifying and addressing potential bugs. Additionally, game developers can encourage players to report any bugs they encounter and work quickly to address and fix those bugs through software updates and patches.

Ensuring the Game is User-Friendly: Testing helps ensure that the game is user-friendly and easy to use, resulting in a more enjoyable experience for players.

To assure a game is user-friendly, game developers can incorporate user interface (UI) and user experience (UX) design principles into their game design. This means creating intuitive controls and menus, designing clear and easy-to-understand tutorials, and providing helpful feedback to players. Game testers can also provide feedback on the game's user-friendliness during testing phases.

Additionally, developers can conduct user testing with real players to identify any pain points or areas for improvement in the game's usability. Overall, prioritizing user-friendliness can greatly enhance a player's enjoyment of the game and improve its overall success.

Ensuring the Game Meets Performance Requirements: Testing helps ensure that the game meets the required performance standards, such as frame rates and loading times. By optimizing the game's performance, developers can create a more enjoyable experience for players.

To ensure a game meets performance requirements, game developers and testers perform various types of testing, such as load testing, stress testing, and performance profiling.

Load testing involves simulating heavy user traffic to test the game's performance under high loads.

Stress testing aims to push the game beyond its limits to see how it performs under extreme conditions.

Performance profiling is used to analyze and optimize the game's code to identify any performance bottlenecks. By conducting these tests, developers can identify and fix performance issues to ensure that the game runs smoothly and meets the performance requirements.

Ensuring the Game Meets Quality Standards: Testing ensures that the game meets the required quality standards, including graphics, sound, and gameplay. By meeting these standards, developers can create a game that is of high quality and enjoyable for players.

Video game testing plays a critical role in game development, ensuring that games are of high quality, bug-free, and meet the expectations of players.

By testing the game thoroughly and addressing any issues, developers can create a game that is fun, engaging, and enjoyable for players, resulting in a positive reputation, increased sales, and success in the gaming industry.

Releasing a game that meets quality standards means that the game has been tested thoroughly and is free from bugs, glitches, or other technical issues that could negatively impact the player's experience.

The game must also meet the desired level of performance, be user-friendly, and provide an enjoyable gaming experience. In addition, the game should meet the artistic and creative vision of the development team and provide a high level of visual and audio quality.

Overall, meeting quality standards ensures that the game meets or exceeds industry and consumer expectations and will be well-received upon its release.

The Testing Process

The video game testing process involves several stages, starting with planning and ending with the final release of the game. The stages of the testing process include:

Planning: In this stage, the testing team develops a testing plan, outlining the objectives, scope, and timelines for the testing process.

Example timeline for a video game testing process:

- **Pre-Alpha testing:** 2-4 weeks
- **Alpha testing:** 4-6 weeks
- **Beta testing:** 4-8 weeks
- **Release candidate testing:** 1-2 weeks
- **Post-release testing:** Ongoing

Keep in mind that these timelines can vary depending on the size and complexity of the game, as well as the resources available for testing. It's important to have a flexible timeline that allows for unexpected issues or delays that may arise during the testing process.

Test Case Development: In this stage, the testing team develops test cases, which are step-by-step instructions for testing the game's different features and functions.

Here is an example of a test case for a video game to test the main players movement:

Test case ID: G001
Test case name: Player movement

Test Steps:

1. Launch the game and select the 'New Game' option.
2. Verify that the game starts at the beginning with the

player in a stationary position.

3. Use the keyboard controls to move the player character forward, backward, left and right.
4. Verify that the player moves in the correct direction and speed in response to the controls.
5. Attempt to jump and verify that the player character jumps to the correct height and distance.
6. Verify that the player character can move smoothly without any lag or glitches.
7. Repeat the test with different characters if the game has multiple characters.
8. Repeat the test with different environments or levels if the game has multiple levels.

Expected Results:

- The player character moves smoothly and responds correctly to the controls.
- The player character jumps to the correct height and distance.
- The game does not lag or glitch during movement.
- The test passes for all characters and levels tested.

Actual Results:

- The player character moves smoothly and responds correctly to the controls.
- The player character jumps to the correct height and distance.
- The game does not lag or glitch during movement.
- The test passes for all characters and levels tested.

Here is another example of a test case for checking the game mechanics of a first person shooter game:

Test case ID: FPS001
Title: Test Case for Shooting Mechanic

Description: This test case is designed to ensure the shooting mechanic of the game is functioning as expected.

Pre-conditions:
- The game is loaded and ready to play.
- The player character has a weapon equipped.

Test Steps:
1. Move the player character to an open area.
2. Aim the weapon at a target, preferably a stationary object such as a box.
3. Fire the weapon using the primary fire button.
4. Observe the trajectory of the bullet and the impact on the target.
5. Move to a different location and repeat steps 2-4.
6. Switch to a different weapon and repeat steps 2-4.

Expected Result:
- The bullet should travel in a straight line from the weapon to the target and create an impact where it hits.
- The impact should be realistic and proportional to the type of weapon used.
- Switching between weapons should be seamless and not cause any glitches or delays.

Actual Result:
- If the expected results match the actual results, the test case passes.
- If any discrepancies are found, the tester should report them as defects and follow up with further testing and verification after the issue is fixed.

Test Execution: In this stage, the testing team executes the test cases and identifies any issues or defects in the game.

Bug Reporting: In this stage, the testing team reports any issues or defects identified during the testing process to the development team, including detailed descriptions of the problem and steps to reproduce the issue.

Here is an example of how a game tester would report and record a bug:

Bug Title: Player falls through the floor

Steps to Reproduce:
1. Start the game and load the "Level 1" map.
2. Move the player character to the edge of the platform.
3. Jump to the adjacent platform.
4. While in the air, move the character to the left.

Expected Result:
The player character should land safely on the adjacent platform.

Actual Result:
The player character falls through the floor and disappears from view.

Severity: High

Notes:
- This bug occurs consistently every time the above steps are followed.
- The bug occurs only in Level 1, and not in any other levels.
- The game physics seem to be causing the issue.
- The bug prevents players from progressing through the game and can lead to frustration and negative user experience.

The game tester would then submit this bug report to the development team through a bug tracking system or software, including all the relevant details and any additional notes or observations they have made. The development team would then investigate the bug and work on fixing it before the game is released to the public.

Bug Fixing: In this stage, the development team fixes the identified issues and defects.

The bug fixing stage is a critical part of the game development process where the development team works to address any issues or defects found during testing. This stage involves analyzing the reported bugs, identifying the root cause of the problem, and developing solutions to fix them.

The development team will then test these fixes to ensure that they have resolved the issue and that the game continues to function properly. Effective bug fixing can lead to a more stable and enjoyable gaming experience for players, making it a crucial aspect of game development.

Regression Testing: In this stage, the testing team retests previously fixed issues to ensure that they are resolved and that the game still functions correctly.

Regression Testing is a crucial step in the game development process. After fixing bugs and issues in the game, the testing team needs to retest the previously resolved problems to make sure they are completely fixed and that the game still works properly. This testing helps ensure that the fixes have not caused any new issues and that the game is stable and meets the desired quality standards.

The aim of regression testing is to make sure that the game is consistent and stable in terms of functionality and performance, providing the best possible experience for the players.

Final Testing: In this stage, the testing team performs final testing to ensure that the game is ready for release.

Final testing is a crucial stage in the game testing process as it ensures that the game is ready for release. The testing team will thoroughly test the game to ensure that all bugs and issues have been resolved, the game is stable, and it meets all performance and quality standards.

This stage also includes verifying that all requested changes and updates have been made and that the game is user-friendly. Once this final testing is complete, and any remaining issues are resolved, the game is ready for release to the public.

Testing Techniques

The main duty of a video game tester is to guarantee the game's excellence and compliance with the required standards before its public release. As a tester, your role involves identifying any game issues or defects and providing valuable feedback to the development team. To thrive in this position, attention to detail, strong communication skills, and comprehension of the game development process are indispensable.

It is crucial to be able to spot even the minutest problems and convey them clearly to the development team. Additionally, familiarity with diverse testing techniques and methodologies is essential for testers to excel in the dynamic game development industry.

There are several testing techniques used in video game testing which include:

Manual Testing: Manual testing involves the tester playing the game and identifying any issues or defects.

Let's say that a game tester is testing a first-person shooter game. One of the areas that the tester needs to focus on is the game's controls, specifically the aiming and shooting mechanics. To perform this test, the tester will manually play through the game and shoot at targets to check for any issues or defects in the controls.

They may also test the controls in different scenarios, such as when the player is moving or jumping, to ensure that the controls remain responsive and accurate. The tester will then document any issues or defects that they find and report them to the development team for further investigation and resolution.

This is an example of manual testing, where the tester manually plays the game and performs specific tests to identify and report any issues or defects.

Automated Testing: Automated testing employs specialized software tools to execute testing tasks, including performance testing and regression testing.

This form of testing often involves creating a script that emulates a player's actions within the game, such as character movement, object interactions, and quest completion. The script can then be automated, with the testing software documenting any encountered issues throughout the process.

Automated testing proves highly advantageous for repetitive tasks that can be automated, freeing up the testing team to focus on more intricate and nuanced testing endeavors. It expedites the testing process and aids in the prompt identification of potential issues.

For instance, in game testing, one repetitive task that can be automated is checking for collisions between the player character and objects within various game levels. By simulating the character's movements and collisions, automated testing enables testers to swiftly pinpoint any bugs or issues without manually repeating the same actions time and again.

Exploratory Testing: Exploratory testing involves testing the game in an unscripted and ad-hoc manner, allowing the tester to discover issues that may not have been identified in the test cases.

In this type of testing, the tester uses their own knowledge, experience, and intuition to find issues that may not be found through other forms of testing.

An example of exploratory testing in a video game context would be for the tester to try out different combinations of weapons and tactics to see how they affect the game's AI and physics engine.

The tester may try to break the game by performing unexpected actions, such as jumping off a building, and see how the game responds. Through this process, the tester may identify issues that were not caught through scripted testing or automated testing.

Usability Testing: Usability testing encompasses evaluating the user interface of the game to ensure its user-friendliness and intuitive nature.

As a vital aspect of a game tester's role, usability testing involves assessing various elements such as menu navigation, control scheme, and visual design. Testers scrutinize the game's menus to determine if they are easily understandable and user-friendly, while also evaluating the ease of learning and operating the control scheme.

Furthermore, the overall visual design and layout of the game are examined to ascertain their user-friendliness and aesthetic appeal. The valuable feedback gathered from usability testing aids developers in enhancing the game's user experience and identifying areas that require improvement.

Load Testing: Load testing involves testing the game under heavy load, such as a large number of players or high traffic on the server.

An example of load testing for a game tester would be to simulate a large number of players in a multiplayer game, such as a battle royale game, to test the game's server performance and response times.

The tester would monitor the game's performance under the load, such as checking for lag or delays in gameplay, and provide feedback to the development team. Load testing is crucial to ensure that a game can handle the expected number of players and activities without crashing or slowing down.

Localization Testing: Localization testing involves testing the game's translation and cultural adaptation for different regions and languages.

An example of localization testing for a game tester would be to test the game's subtitles and audio to ensure that they are translated correctly and that they match the lip movements of characters.

The tester would also evaluate the game's text and make sure that it is culturally appropriate for different regions. Localization testing can help ensure that the game is accessible and enjoyable for players from different regions and backgrounds.

Video game testing is a critical part of the game development process, ensuring that games are of high quality and ready for release to the public. By following the testing process, understanding the role of a tester, and using different testing techniques, video game testers can ensure that the game is of the highest quality and provides an enjoyable gaming experience for players.

CHAPTER 3 –
THE DIFFERENT
STAGES OF GAME
DEVELOPMENT

The process of game development is a multifaceted and iterative journey, comprising distinct stages, each presenting its unique challenges and prerequisites. In the upcoming chapter, we will delve into the various phases of game development, encompassing everything from the initial concept to the final release.

Concept

In the concept stage, the foundation of the game idea is laid. This phase involves ideation and brainstorming to create an innovative and captivating game concept that will engage players. The team produces a Game Design Document (GDD) during this stage, which outlines the essential mechanics, storyline, characters, and environment of the game. The GDD acts as a roadmap for the entire development process.

Pre-Production

The pre-production stage is where the game's development begins to take shape. During this stage, the team works on creating prototypes, storyboards, and mockups to test the game's mechanics and visualize the game's world. This stage is critical for identifying and resolving any issues with the game design before moving into production.

Production

The production stage is where the game is built. The team creates the game's assets, including character models, textures, sound effects, and music. The game's code is written, and the mechanics are programmed. This stage is where the bulk of the work happens, and it can take several months or even years to complete.

Testing

The testing stage is where the game is put through its paces to identify and eliminate any bugs and glitches. This stage involves both internal testing by the development team and external testing by beta testers and focus groups. Testing is essential for ensuring the game is stable, reliable, and enjoyable for players.

Release

The release stage is where the game is launched to the public. This stage involves creating marketing materials, submitting the game to distribution platforms, and setting a release date. The release stage is crucial for creating buzz and generating interest in the game.

Post-Release

The post-release stage is where the game is supported after launch. This stage involves monitoring player feedback and addressing any issues that arise through patches and updates. The post-release stage is critical for maintaining the game's popularity and keeping players engaged.

Game development is a complex and iterative process that involves many stages, from concept to release. Each stage is essential for creating a high-quality game that is stable, enjoyable, and meets the expectations of players. By understanding the different stages of game development, developers can ensure that their game is successful and well-received by the gaming community.

The Role of Testers in Each Stage of the Game Development Process

Ensuring a game is stable, enjoyable, and meets player expectations is crucial to game development, and testers play a vital role in achieving these goals. This chapter will delve into the various stages of game development and the essential contributions of testers in each stage.

Concept Stage

During the concept stage, testers play a crucial role in providing feedback on the game's design document. Testers can identify any potential issues with the game's mechanics, storyline, characters, and world, which can be addressed before moving into pre-production.

Pre-Production Stage

In the pre-production stage, testers work closely with the development team to create prototypes and mockups. Testers can provide feedback on the game's mechanics and visuals, identifying any issues that need to be addressed before moving into production.

Production Stage

During the production stage, testers play a critical role in ensuring the stability and functionality of the game. Testers can identify and report any bugs or glitches, which can be fixed before the game is released to the public.

Testing Stage

In the testing stage, testers play a critical role in identifying and eliminating any bugs and glitches. Testers can provide feedback on the game's mechanics, controls, difficulty, and overall gameplay experience. Testers can also help identify any potential exploits or balance issues that need to be addressed before the game is released.

Release Stage
During the release stage, testers play a critical role in ensuring that the game is stable and reliable for players. Testers can provide feedback on any issues that arise during the launch, such as server crashes, game-breaking bugs, or compatibility issues.

Post-Release Stage
In the post-release phase, testers hold a vital position in supporting the game after its launch. They actively monitor player feedback and pinpoint any issues requiring attention through patches and updates. Additionally, testers contribute valuable insights on new features and content, guaranteeing the game's ongoing engagement and enjoyment for players.

Throughout the game development process, testers assume a critical role in ensuring game stability, enjoyment, and alignment with player expectations. From offering feedback on the design document to identifying and rectifying bugs and glitches during testing, testers play a pivotal role in each development stage.

By closely collaborating with the development team, testers significantly contribute to the game's success and its reception within the gaming community.

The Importance of Communication and Collaboration for Video Game Testers

In the context of video game testing, communication and collaboration are vital skills that testers must possess. This chapter delves into the significance of communication and collaboration in video game testing, and how testers can enhance their competencies in these aspects.

Communication

Effective communication is crucial for testers to provide valuable feedback on the game's mechanics, controls, and overall gameplay experience. Testers must possess the ability to convey their findings and observations to the development team in a clear and accurate manner, which is essential for the game's quality and success.

Good communication involves being clear, concise, and specific. Testers should use precise language when reporting issues, providing feedback, and suggesting improvements. They should also be able to describe their experiences in detail, including any issues or bugs they encounter.

In addition to communicating effectively with the development team, testers should also be able to communicate with other testers. Collaboration between testers can help identify and address issues more quickly, leading to a more stable and enjoyable game.

Collaboration

Collaboration is essential for video game testers to work effectively with the development team and other testers. Testers should be able to work together to identify and address issues, share feedback and suggestions, and help improve the game's overall quality.

Effective collaboration involves being open-minded, respectful, and supportive. Testers should be willing to listen to others' opinions, provide constructive feedback, and work together to find solutions to problems.

Collaboration can take many forms, including sharing feedback and suggestions through online platforms or participating in beta testing and focus groups. Testers can also collaborate by sharing resources, such as tools or guides, that can help them identify and address issues more efficiently.

Benefits of Communication and Collaboration

Effective communication and collaboration can bring many benefits to video game testers. By communicating effectively, testers can ensure that their feedback is clear, concise, and specific, leading to a better understanding of the issues and a more efficient process for addressing them.

Collaboration can help testers work more effectively together, identifying issues more quickly and sharing feedback and suggestions. Collaboration can also help testers feel more connected and engaged with the development team and other testers, leading to a more positive and supportive working environment.

Communication and collaboration are critical skills for video game testers. Effective communication can help testers provide clear, concise, and specific feedback to the development team, while collaboration can help testers work together to identify and address issues more efficiently. By improving their communication and collaboration skills, video game testers can help improve the quality of the game and create a more positive and supportive working environment.

CHAPTER 4 - TYPES OF VIDEO GAME TESTING

Video game testing holds immense significance within the game development process, as it ensures high-quality standards and delivers an exceptional gaming experience for players. Game testers can undertake various types of testing to accomplish these goals. In the following chapter, we delve into the diverse types of video game testing and their respective roles in the development journey.

Functional Testing

Functional testing serves as the fundamental form of testing, employed to verify the proper operation of the game's features and functions. It entails assessing the game's adherence to intended gameplay, including menu navigation, game mechanics, and gameplay elements. The primary objective of functional testing is to identify and address any potential issues or bugs that could impact the game's playability and overall user experience.

Performance Testing

Performance testing is used to ensure that the game runs smoothly and is optimized for performance on a variety of devices. This testing involves checking that the game can handle high volumes of data, such as character models, animations, and special effects, without slowing down or crashing. Performance testing also involves ensuring that the game runs well on different hardware configurations, including consoles, PCs, and mobile devices.

Compatibility Testing

Compatibility testing is used to ensure that the game can be played on different platforms and hardware configurations. This testing involves checking that the game is compatible with different operating systems, browsers, and graphics cards. Compatibility testing is essential to ensure that the game can reach the widest possible audience and is not limited to a single platform.

Localization Testing

Localization testing is used to ensure that the game can be played in different languages and cultural contexts. This testing involves checking that the game's text, audio, and graphics are translated correctly and make sense in different languages. Localization testing is important to ensure that the game is accessible to players around the world and that it provides a consistent and enjoyable experience regardless of the player's language or cultural background.

User Acceptance Testing

User acceptance testing (UAT) serves as the conclusive phase of testing, where real players take part. Its aim is to assess whether the game fulfils players' expectations and delivers an exceptional gaming experience. UAT encompasses diverse testing approaches like focus groups, surveys, and play-testing. This stage's purpose is to guarantee the game's enjoyment and engagement for players while identifying and resolving any remaining issues before its official release.

Video game testing is a crucial part of the game development process, and there are several types of testing that video game testers can perform. Functional testing, performance testing, compatibility testing, localization testing, and user acceptance testing are all important types of testing that can ensure that the game is of high quality and provides a great gaming experience for players.

By performing these types of testing, video game testers can help ensure that the game is successful and well-received by players.

Functional Testing for
Video Game Testers

What is Functional Testing?

Functional testing focuses on verifying that the game's features and functions operate as intended. It encompasses examining menus, game mechanics, and gameplay elements to ensure their proper functioning. The primary objective of functional testing is to detect any potential issues or bugs that could impact the game's playability and overall user experience.

Functional testing is commonly conducted during the initial phases of game development and persists throughout the entire development process. Its ongoing implementation helps maintain the quality and functionality of the game, ensuring a smooth and enjoyable gaming experience.

Functional Testing Techniques

There are several techniques that video game testers can use to perform functional testing. These techniques include:

Test Case Creation

Creating test cases is an effective way to ensure that all of the game's features and functions are tested thoroughly. Test cases are sets of instructions that testers follow to test specific areas of the game. Test cases can be created for menus, game mechanics, and gameplay elements, and they should be created based on the game's design and requirements.

Boundary Testing

Boundary testing involves testing the limits of the game's features and functions. This testing ensures that the game can handle extreme situations, such as high scores or character levels, without crashing or encountering issues. Boundary testing is important to ensure that the game is robust and can handle unexpected situations.

An example of boundary testing for a game tester could involve testing the upper limits of a character's level in a role-playing game. The tester could try to level up the character to the maximum level allowed in the game and see if any issues or glitches occur. The tester could also try to achieve the highest score possible in a particular level or challenge and see if the game can handle the increased data and processing requirements without any problems.

Compatibility Testing

Compatibility testing involves evaluating the game's features and functionalities across diverse hardware configurations and operating systems. Its primary goal is to ensure seamless gameplay on a wide range of devices, maximizing accessibility for players.

For game testers, an instance of compatibility testing would involve assessing the game's performance on various consoles or devices, such as PlayStation, Xbox, and PC, to ensure smooth operation without compatibility issues. Additionally, the tester would test the game on different operating systems like Windows, Mac, and Linux, to verify its compatibility across multiple platforms.

Regression Testing

Regression testing involves testing the game's features and functions after changes have been made to the game's code or design. This testing ensures that changes do not cause new issues or bugs to appear in the game. Regression testing is important to ensure that the game remains stable and playable throughout the development process.

Ad-Hoc Testing

Ad-hoc testing involves testing the game's features and functions in an informal and unstructured manner. This testing can be useful for identifying issues or bugs that may not be discovered through structured testing techniques. Ad-hoc testing is often performed by experienced testers who can identify potential issues quickly and efficiently.

Functional testing is a critical part of video game testing, and video game testers must perform it effectively to ensure that the game is of high quality and provides a great gaming experience for players.

Test case creation, boundary testing, compatibility testing, regression testing, and ad-hoc testing are all effective techniques that video game testers can use to perform functional testing. By performing functional testing effectively, video game testers can help ensure that the game is successful and well-received by players.

Compatibility Testing for
Games Testers

What is Compatibility Testing?

Compatibility testing assesses the game's smooth performance on various hardware configurations and software versions. Its importance lies in maximizing accessibility to players, regardless of their device or operating system.

Compatibility Testing Techniques

There are several techniques that games testers can use to perform compatibility testing.
These techniques include:

Hardware Compatibility Testing

Hardware compatibility testing involves testing the game on different hardware configurations, such as different processors, graphics cards, and memory capacities. This testing ensures that the game can run smoothly on a variety of hardware setups without encountering any issues.

As an example, assume that a game developer has created a new game that is designed to run on PC. As a games tester, your task is to ensure that the game runs smoothly on different PC configurations, including both low-end and high-end machines.

To perform Hardware Compatibility Testing, you would:

- Collect a variety of PC configurations with different hardware components, such as graphics cards, processors, and RAM.

- Install the game on each PC configuration and run the game to ensure that it functions properly.

- Test the game on different display resolutions and monitor sizes to ensure that the game is compatible with a wide range of display configurations.

- Verify that the game runs smoothly without any issues, such as crashes, freezes, or graphical glitches, on each PC configuration.

- Make sure to write down any problems or issues that come up during testing and let the development team know about them so they can be fixed.

Operating System Compatibility Testing

The process of operating system compatibility testing entails evaluating the game's performance on various operating systems, including Windows, MacOS, and Linux. This meticulous testing guarantees a seamless gameplay experience across different platforms by identifying and addressing any compatibility issues that may arise.

Operating System Compatibility Testing involves rigorously assessing the features and functionalities of a game to ensure their smooth operation across diverse operating systems, such as Windows, macOS, and Linux. This form of testing holds immense importance as different operating systems possess distinct settings and configurations that can impact the game's performance. By conducting comprehensive operating system compatibility testing, potential issues can be detected and resolved, ensuring optimal gameplay across various platforms.

As a games tester, you will need to test the game on each operating system to identify any issues that may arise. This includes testing the game's installation process, graphics, sound, controls, and overall gameplay experience. You will also need to ensure that the game runs smoothly on different resolutions and aspect ratios.

To perform this testing, you may need to have access to multiple computers or virtual machines running different operating systems. Once you've identified any issues, you'll need to document them and report them to the development team for resolution. The team may need to make adjustments to the game's code or design to ensure that it works correctly on each operating system.

Network Compatibility Testing

Network compatibility testing involves testing the game's network features, such as multiplayer and online gameplay, on different network configurations and speeds. This testing ensures that the game's online features can function correctly on different network setups without encountering any issues.

It's a type of testing performed by game testers to ensure that a game can function properly in different network environments. For example, testers may simulate low network bandwidth, high latency, or packet loss to ensure that the game can still function without issues.

During Network Compatibility Testing, game testers verify that the game's network features, such as multiplayer modes and online connectivity, are working as intended. They also ensure that the game can handle a variety of network configurations, such as different routers, firewalls, and NAT types.

In addition to testing the game's network functionality, testers may also evaluate the game's performance and stability under different network conditions. For example, they may test the game's behaviour when the network connection is interrupted or when the player's device switches from Wi-Fi to mobile data.

Any issues or bugs discovered during Network Compatibility Testing are documented and reported to the development team for resolution.

Peripheral Compatibility Testing

Peripheral compatibility testing involves testing the game with different peripherals, such as game controllers, keyboards, and mice. This testing ensures that the game can be played with a variety of peripherals without encountering any issues.

It's a type of testing performed by game testers to ensure that the game can work with various peripheral devices, such as controllers, keyboards, and mice. This type of testing involves connecting different types of peripherals to the game and ensuring that they work as intended.

For example, if a game is designed to work with a specific type of controller, peripheral compatibility testing involves testing the game with other controllers to ensure that the game can be played with different controllers without encountering any issues. The game tester would test the buttons, triggers, and joysticks of the controller to ensure that they work as expected in the game.

Peripheral compatibility testing is important to ensure that the game can be played with a wide range of peripheral devices, which can improve the overall user experience. By testing the compatibility of different peripherals, game testers can ensure that players can use the peripherals they prefer and still have an enjoyable gaming experience.

Localization Compatibility Testing
Localization compatibility testing involves testing the game's compatibility with different languages, fonts, and text directions. This testing ensures that the game can be played and understood by players who speak different languages.

It's a crucial step for ensuring that a video game is suitable for players in different regions of the world. The goal of this testing is to verify that the game's interface, graphics, and text can be displayed and understood correctly in different languages, cultures, and regions.

During Localization Compatibility Testing, the games tester would perform the following tasks:

- Install the game in the target language: The tester

would install the game in the language that is specific to the region or country where the game will be played.

- Verify the game's language settings: The tester would verify that the game's language settings are set to the correct language for the target region or country.

- Test the game's fonts and graphics: The tester would verify that the game's fonts and graphics can be displayed correctly in the target language and that they are culturally appropriate for the target region.

- Test the game's text: The tester would verify that the game's text is accurately translated and localized for the target language, and that it is appropriate for the target region.

- Test the game's audio: The tester would verify that the game's audio can be played correctly in the target language and that it is appropriate for the target region.

- Test the game's cultural sensitivity: The tester would verify that the game's content and gameplay are appropriate and sensitive to the cultural norms and values of the target region.

Through the execution of Localization Compatibility Testing, game testers contribute to the assurance of an enjoyable and immersive gaming experience for players across various regions of the world.

In general, compatibility testing holds immense significance within the realm of video game testing, and it is imperative for game testers to conduct this process efficiently to maximize the game's accessibility to a wide player base. By effectively conducting compatibility testing, game testers play a crucial role in ensuring that the game remains accessible to players worldwide, ultimately delivering a phenomenal gaming experience.

Performance Testing for
Games Testers

Performance testing is an important aspect of video game testing that focuses on ensuring the game performs optimally under a variety of conditions.

What is Performance Testing?

Performance testing involves testing the game's performance under different scenarios to ensure that it runs smoothly and does not encounter any performance-related issues. Performance testing is crucial because it ensures that the game provides players with a smooth and enjoyable gaming experience.

Performance Testing Techniques

There are several techniques that games testers can use to perform performance testing. These techniques include:

Load Testing

Load testing involves testing the game's performance under heavy load conditions, such as a large number of players or high traffic volume. This testing ensures that the game can handle high traffic and player volumes without encountering any performance-related issues.

Load testing is a crucial step in ensuring that a multiplayer game can handle a large number of players at once for example. By simulating a high volumes of virtual players, a tester can identify any potential issues that may arise during gameplay. This testing involves creating multiple virtual machines and connecting them to the game server to simulate multiple players playing the game simultaneously.

The tester would then closely monitor the game's performance under heavy load to ensure that it remains stable and doesn't crash. They would also look for any lag or latency issues that may affect gameplay, as well as any issues related to server response time. This testing can help identify any potential issues related to the game's scalability and provide insight into necessary changes to improve the game's performance under heavy load.

In short, load testing ensures that the game can handle the maximum number of players without crashing or experiencing performance issues, which ultimately enhances the player experience.

Stress Testing

Stress testing involves testing the game's performance under extreme conditions, such as running the game on low-end hardware or with limited memory. This testing ensures that the game can run smoothly even on low-end hardware and does not crash or encounter any performance-related issues.

Imagine you're a games tester for a thrilling new action-packed video game that requires lightning-fast reflexes and intense gameplay. As part of your testing process, you'll need to put the game under extreme stress to see how it performs.

One way to do this is by creating a challenging scenario where the player is bombarded by multiple enemies and the environment is constantly changing. You might increase the number of enemies on the screen or create a situation where the player is surrounded by explosions and other hazards.

During the stress testing, you'll closely monitor the game's performance to see if it remains stable and responsive. You'll also keep an eye out for any issues related to graphics, sound, or gameplay mechanics, and document any problems you come across.

Stress testing is an important part of game testing, as it helps to reveal any vulnerabilities or limitations in the game's design. The ultimate objective of stress testing is to enable the development team to make the necessary modifications and improvements to the game's performance under high-pressure situations.

By conducting stress tests, you can assist in ensuring that the game provides players with a challenging yet enjoyable experience, regardless of the intensity of the gameplay.

Soak Testing

Soak testing involves testing the game's performance over an extended period to ensure that it can perform consistently without any issues. This testing is particularly important for online games, where players may play for extended periods.

Let's say you are a games tester for an upcoming multiplayer racing game that involves long races lasting over an hour. As part of your testing process, you would perform soak testing to see how the game holds up over an extended period of time.

To do this, you would start a race and let the game run for several hours, constantly monitoring the game's performance, such as frame rate, server response time, and player synchronization. You would also perform actions in the game, such as accelerating, braking, and turning to see if any issues arise over time.

During the soak testing, you would look for any issues related to memory leaks or resource utilization that could impact the game's performance over time. You would also monitor the game's stability and check for any bugs or crashes that may occur during extended gameplay.

The goal of soak testing is to identify any issues related to the game's stability and performance over time, so that the development team can make necessary changes to improve the game's performance and ensure that it remains playable for extended periods.

By performing soak testing, you can help ensure that the game is enjoyable and engaging for players, even during long gameplay sessions.

Compatibility Testing

Compatibility testing is also a type of performance testing. By testing the game on different hardware configurations and operating systems, games testers can ensure that the game runs smoothly on a variety of platforms without encountering any performance-related issues.

Let's say you're testing a new game that's going to be released on both PC and Xbox. As part of the compatibility testing process, you would test the game's features and functions on both platforms to ensure that the game runs smoothly and without any issues on each one.

To do this, you would first test the game on a PC with different hardware configurations and operating systems to ensure that it works properly on a variety of setups. This might include testing the game on a Windows 10 PC with an Intel processor, as well as testing it on a Windows 7 PC with an AMD processor, to ensure that it runs smoothly on different configurations.

You would also test the game on Xbox, ensuring that it runs without any issues on different versions of the console, such as the Xbox One and Xbox Series X/S. This would involve testing the game on each console to ensure that it works properly, and checking that all the game's features are accessible and function as expected.

Throughout the testing process, you would document any issues or bugs you encounter, and report them to the development team for resolution. This type of testing will ensure that the game is accessible to as many players as possible and provide a smooth experience for gamers on different platforms.

Graphical Testing

Graphical testing involves testing the game's performance under different graphical settings, such as high, medium, and low. This testing ensures that the game can run smoothly on a variety of graphical settings without encountering any performance-related issues.

As a game tester, you may be tasked with conducting graphical testing to ensure that the game's graphics meet the required standards. This type of testing involves checking the game's visuals, including textures, lighting, shadows, and other visual effects, to ensure that they are rendered correctly and appear as intended.

For example, you may need to verify that the textures used in the game are not pixelated or blurry and are rendered with appropriate resolutions. You would also check that the lighting and shadows in the game are consistent and don't flicker or disappear unexpectedly.

During graphical testing, you may also need to check that the game runs smoothly at different graphics settings, including high and low graphics settings. This helps to ensure that the game can be played on a variety of different hardware configurations without experiencing issues.

You would need to document any issues or glitches you encounter during graphical testing and report them to the development team for resolution. By conducting thorough graphical testing, you can help to ensure that the game looks visually appealing and engaging for players, while also maintaining stable and consistent graphics performance.

Overall, performance testing is an essential aspect of video game testing, and games testers must perform it effectively to ensure that the game provides players with a smooth and enjoyable gaming experience. Load testing, stress testing, soak testing, compatibility testing, and graphical testing are all effective techniques that games testers can use to perform performance testing.

By conducting performance testing effectively, games testers can help ensure that the game performs optimally under a variety of conditions and provides players with a great gaming experience.

Localisation Testing for
Games Testers

Localisation testing involves testing the game's functionality and content in different languages, cultures, and regions to ensure that it meets the needs of players in those regions. This testing ensures that the game's text, audio, and graphics are culturally relevant and that players can understand and enjoy the game regardless of their language or cultural background.

Localisation Testing Techniques

There are several techniques that games testers can use to perform localisation testing. These techniques include:

Language Testing

Language testing involves testing the game's text and audio in different languages to ensure that it is correctly translated and that players can understand the content. Games testers should check for grammatical errors, incorrect translations, and issues with font size and readability.

Example of a language test being carried out:

Game: "Fantasy Quest"

Role: Language Tester

==== Test Scenario ====

Imagine you're a language tester for the amazing game "Fantasy Quest"! Your main job is to make sure that the game's text and dialogue are spot on, making the game enjoyable for players around the world. Let's walk through an example of how you'd test the language aspect of the game in a fun and detailed way:

1. Test Objective

- Let's check if the subtitles for a specific quest are accurate.

2. Test Setup
- Start playing the game and go to the quest we want to test.

- Change the game language to the one we're testing (let's say Spanish).

3.Test Execution
- Read the quest objectives and dialogue carefully, comparing them with the original language (let's say English).

- Keep an eye out for any grammar or spelling mistakes in the subtitles and dialogues.

- Make sure the subtitles match what the characters are saying and appear at the right time.

- Pay attention to cultural references and expressions, making sure they're translated well and make sense in the target language.

- Check that any written texts in the game, like signs, menus, or item descriptions, are translated accurately.

4. Test Documentation
- Write down any issues or inconsistencies you find, and be sure to explain them clearly so the developers can understand.

- If possible, take screenshots or make videos to show specific problems you come across.

- Share any suggestions you have for improvements or alternative translations that could make the game even better.

5. Test Reporting
- Put together a report with all the issues you found,

organized by importance and how they could affect gameplay and the player's experience.

- Send the report to the game's development team or project manager, making sure to explain everything and offer suggestions for fixing the problems.

6. Retest and Follow-up

- After the developers have made the necessary changes, play through the quest again to see if the issues have been resolved.

- Check that the modifications match what was intended and accurately convey the meaning in the target language.

- Keep in touch with the development team to give them feedback on the changes and address any other concerns or questions you might have.

By conducting thorough language testing, you're helping make "Fantasy Quest" an incredible game that can be enjoyed by players all over the world! Your attention to detail and dedication to improving the game's localization will truly enhance the gaming experience for everyone.

Cultural Testing

Cultural testing involves testing the game's content and graphics to ensure that they are culturally appropriate and relevant to players in different regions. Games testers should check for issues such as offensive content, cultural insensitivity, and incorrect cultural references.

Example of a cultural test being carried out:

Game: "Quest of Legends"

Objective: To assess the cultural representation and sensitivity of a fantasy role-playing game called "Quest of Legends."

==== Test Scenario ====

1. Research and Preparation

- The game tester gathers information about the cultures represented in the game. In this case, "Quest of Legends" features diverse fictional cultures inspired by real-world counterparts.

- The tester familiarizes themselves with the customs, traditions, and historical background of each culture to ensure accurate representation.

2. Character and Dialogue Assessment

- The tester selects characters from different cultures within the game and reviews their dialogue, speeches, and interactions.

- They evaluate whether the character's language, mannerisms, and behaviour align with the cultural norms they represent.

- The tester looks for any instances of cultural appropriation, stereotypes, or offensive language that might unintentionally misrepresent a particular culture.

3. Environmental and Artistic Elements

- The tester explores the game world, paying attention to the environmental design, architecture, and visual aesthetics of each culture's region.

- They assess whether the art style and representations accurately reflect the cultural inspiration without perpetuating stereotypes or being culturally insensitive.

- The tester examines any cultural symbols, artefacts, or historical references within the game and ensures they are appropriately contextualized and respectful.

4. Gameplay Mechanics and Quests

- The tester engages in quests, missions, or scenarios related to different cultures.

- They evaluate if the objectives, challenges, and rewards align with the cultural themes and values being portrayed.

- The tester checks for any instances where gameplay mechanics might reinforce cultural biases or inaccurately represent a culture's practices.

5. Feedback and Reporting

- Throughout the test, the tester takes detailed notes, screenshots, and records any problematic elements they encounter.

- They compile a comprehensive report highlighting any cultural issues or sensitivities identified during the test.

- The tester provides suggestions and recommendations on how the game developers can improve cultural representation, avoid stereotypes, and ensure cultural sensitivity.

By conducting a thorough cultural test, the games tester helps ensure that "Quest of Legends" presents its diverse fictional cultures in a respectful and authentic manner.

Compliance Testing

Compliance testing involves testing the game's compliance with regional regulations and standards. Games testers should check for issues such as age ratings, content restrictions, and local laws and regulations.

An example of a compliance test being carried out:

Game: "Space Galaxy Adventures"

Objective: To evaluate if the game "Space Galaxy Adventures" complies with the content guidelines and regulations specified by the Entertainment Software Rating Board (ESRB).

==== **Test Scenario** ====

1. Familiarization
- The tester becomes familiar with the ESRB's guidelines and requirements for different age ratings and content descriptors.

- They review the specific guidelines relevant to the game's genre, themes, and target audience.

2. Content Assessment
- The tester systematically plays through the game's various levels, missions, and story lines.

- They evaluate the game's content for elements such as violence, language, sexual themes, drug use, and other potentially objectionable material.

- The tester ensures that the content aligns with the appropriate age rating, content descriptors, and avoids exceeding the limitations set by the ESRB.

3. User Interface and Accessibility
- The tester reviews the game's user interface (UI) elements, including menus, options, and controls.

- They verify that the UI text, icons, and visuals are clear, legible, and easy to understand.

- The tester checks if the game offers appropriate accessibility features, such as adjustable difficulty levels, colour-blind modes, and customizable controls, as required by accessibility guidelines.

4. Online Interactions and Privacy
- If the game features online multiplayer or social

interactions, the tester assesses the mechanisms for player interactions, chat functions, and user-generated content sharing.

- They ensure that appropriate measures are in place to prevent harassment, protect user privacy, and comply with relevant laws, such as the Children's Online Privacy Protection Act (COPPA) or the General Data Protection Regulation (GDPR).

5. Compliance Reporting

- Throughout the test, the tester meticulously documents any instances where the game deviates from the ESRB guidelines or relevant regulations.

- They compile a detailed report highlighting areas of non-compliance and provide suggestions on how the developers can rectify or improve those aspects.

- The tester may also recommend adjustments to game content, UI elements, or online features to align with the appropriate age rating and compliance standards.

By conducting a thorough compliance test, the games tester ensures that "Space Galaxy Adventures" meets the guidelines and regulations specified by the ESRB, fostering a safe and appropriate gaming experience for the intended audience.

Functionality Testing

Functionality testing involves testing the game's functionality in different languages and regions to ensure that it works correctly and that players can navigate the game without encountering any issues. Games testers should check for issues such as language-specific bugs, incorrect translations, and compatibility issues.

An example of a functionality test being carried out:

Game: "Mystic Dungeon"

Objective: To make sure that everything works smoothly and without any problems in the game "Mystic Dungeon," regardless of the platform (PC, console, mobile) players use.

==== **Test Scenario** ====

1. Getting Started

- We'll install the game on different platforms, like PC, console, or mobile, just following the provided instructions.

- Our goal is to ensure that the installation process is hassle-free and there are no errors or complications.

- Once we launch the game, we'll check if it starts up properly without any crashes or performance issues.

2. Exploring Gameplay

- Let's dive into the tutorial or initial levels, focusing on the basics like moving around, combat, and interacting with objects and characters.

- Our aim is to ensure that all the controls respond well, are accurate, and work exactly as intended.

- We'll be on the lookout for any oddities, glitches, or problems with collision detection, physics, or character animations.

3. Progress and Saving

- As we progress through different levels, stages, or quests, we want to ensure that the game keeps track of our progress correctly.

- We'll check if completed objectives, acquired items, and character statistics are properly saved.

- Saving and loading multiple times, we'll make sure that our progress is safe, with no data corruption or loss.

4. Enjoying Sight and Sound

- We'll pay attention to the game's audio, including background music, sound effects, voice overs, and ambient sounds.

- Our goal is to ensure that the audio elements synchronize well, sound clear, and add to the immersive experience.

- We'll also keep an eye on the visuals, like graphics, textures, lighting, and special effects, looking for any visual glitches, rendering issues, or inconsistencies.

5. Multiplayer and Online Features (if applicable)

- If the game supports multiplayer or online play, we'll join matches, co-op sessions, or interact with the community.

- Our focus will be on testing network stability, responsiveness of online features, and the overall multiplayer experience.

- We'll report any issues related to matchmaking, server stability, latency, or synchronization problems to ensure a smooth online experience.

6. Performance and Optimization

- We want to make sure that the game runs smoothly on different platforms.

- We'll check the frame rate, loading times, and overall responsiveness, ensuring players have a seamless experience.

- Additionally, we'll keep an eye out for any performance-related issues like resource usage, memory leaks, or inefficient code that could affect gameplay.

7. Reporting Bugs

- Throughout our testing, we'll carefully document any bugs, glitches, crashes, or unexpected behaviour we encounter.

- Our reports will include detailed information about how to reproduce each issue, along with screenshots or videos.

- We'll categorize and prioritize the reported issues based on their severity and impact on gameplay.

By conducting this comprehensive functionality test, we aim to ensure that "Mystic Dungeon" delivers a smooth and enjoyable gaming experience for players across different platforms.

User Interface Testing

User interface testing involves testing the game's user interface in different languages and regions to ensure that it is easy to navigate and that players can understand the game's controls and features. Games testers should check for issues such as incorrectly translated menus and controls, incorrect font sizes, and issues with readability.

Example of user interface testing on a game:

Game: "Pixel Quest"

Objective: To evaluate the user interface (UI) of the game "Pixel Quest" and ensure it provides an intuitive and seamless experience for players.

==== Test Scenario ====
1. Navigating Menus

- The tester will explore various menus, such as the main menu, options menu, and in-game pause menu.

- They will check if the menus are easy to navigate, visually appealing, and provide clear options and instructions.

- The tester will verify that all buttons, drop-downs, sliders, and check boxes work as expected.

2. HUD (Heads-Up Display)
- The tester will examine the HUD elements, including health bars, mini-maps, inventory slots, and quest trackers.

- They will ensure that the HUD elements are well-positioned, not obstructive, and provide relevant information to players.

- The tester will confirm that the HUD updates accurately and responds appropriately to changes in gameplay.

3. Control Mapping and Customization
- The tester will review the control scheme and assess whether it is intuitive and easy to learn.

- They will check if players can remap controls to their preference and if the customization options are user-friendly.

- The tester will verify that the control inputs are responsive and accurately correspond to the assigned actions.

4. Tooltips and Tutorials
- The tester will interact with tooltips that provide additional information about in-game objects, abilities, or UI elements.

- They will assess the clarity and usefulness of the tooltips, ensuring they provide relevant guidance to players.

- The tester will evaluate the effectiveness of tutorials

or hints in teaching players game mechanics or UI interactions.

5. Screen Resolutions and Aspect Ratios

- The tester will test the game across different screen resolutions and aspect ratios, including standard and widescreen displays.

- They will verify that the UI elements adapt appropriately to different resolutions without overlapping or getting cut off.

- The tester will ensure that the UI remains readable and visually pleasing across a range of screen configurations.

6. Localization and Language Support

- If the game supports multiple languages, the tester will switch between language options to ensure proper translation and localization.

- They will evaluate if the translated text fits within the UI elements without causing any layout issues or readability problems.

- The tester will confirm that all UI elements, including buttons, labels, and menus, adapt correctly to different languages.

7. Usability and Feedback

- The tester will provide feedback on the overall usability of the UI, suggesting improvements to enhance user experience.

- They will assess factors such as the clarity of icons, font sizes, color schemes, and visual hierarchy of information.

- The tester will report any instances of UI elements that

are misleading, confusing, or lacking proper feedback.

By conducting a comprehensive user interface test, the games tester aims to ensure that "Pixel Quest" delivers an intuitive, visually appealing, and user-friendly UI that enhances the overall gameplay experience.

Localisation testing is an essential aspect of video game testing, and games testers must perform it effectively to ensure that the game meets the needs of players in different languages and cultural contexts. Language testing, cultural testing, compliance testing, functionality testing, and user interface testing are all effective techniques that games testers can use to perform localisation testing.

By performing localisation testing effectively, games testers can help ensure that the game's text, audio, and graphics are culturally relevant and that players can enjoy the game regardless of their language or cultural background.

User Interface Testing
for Games Testers

User interface testing involves testing the game's user interface (UI) to ensure that it is easy to navigate and that players can understand the game's controls and features. This testing ensures that the game's UI is intuitive and easy to use, regardless of the player's experience level.

User Interface Testing Techniques

There are several techniques that games testers can use to perform user interface testing. These techniques include:

Navigation Testing

Navigation testing involves testing the game's menus and controls to ensure that they are easy to navigate and that players can understand how to use them. Games testers should check for issues such as unclear instructions, missing or incorrect icons, and issues with button mapping.

Example of navigation testing being carried out in relation to user interface testing:

Game: "Adventure Legends"

Objective: To evaluate the navigation within the game's user interface (UI), ensuring that players can easily navigate through menus and controls. The focus is on checking for issues such as unclear instructions, missing or incorrect icons, and problems with button mapping.

==== Test Scenario ====
1. Main Menu Navigation

The games tester will thoroughly navigate through the main menu, examining the clarity of instructions provided to players. Assessing if the instructions are clear and easy to understand, ensuring players can navigate through the menu without confusion.

The tester will then verify that important menu options are labeled appropriately, avoiding any ambiguity.

2. In-Game Menu and Pause Navigation

During gameplay, the tester will evaluate the in-game menu and pause navigation. They will also check if the instructions within the menu are concise and guide players effectively, allowing them to navigate without interrupting the game flow.

The tester will then verify that icons representing various options are present and correctly represent their intended functions.

3. Sub-menu Navigation

- The tester will explore different submenus, such as character customization, inventory management, or quest logs.

- They will assess the clarity of instructions provided within these submenus, ensuring players can navigate through different screens with ease.

- The tester will verify that icons and labels used in submenus are clear and accurately represent their respective features or functions.

4. Button and Control Navigation

- The tester will focus on the button mapping and control navigation within the UI.

- They will assess if the button mapping aligns with the expected actions, ensuring players can interact with the game intuitively.

- The tester will verify that instructions for control inputs are accurate and clearly communicated, avoiding any confusion or misinterpretation.

5. Tutorial and Guidance

- The tester will assess the effectiveness of tutorials or guidance provided within the UI to help players understand the game's controls and navigation.

- They will check if the instructions are clear, concise, and provide step-by-step guidance for new players.

- The tester will verify that players can easily understand and follow the instructions to navigate through the game effectively.

6. Usability and Accessibility

- Throughout the navigation test, the tester will consider the overall usability and accessibility of the UI.

- They will assess if the instructions, icons, and button mapping accommodate players with different levels of experience and cater to diverse player needs.

- The tester will provide feedback on any areas where improvements can be made to enhance user experience and ensure clear and intuitive navigation.

By conducting a comprehensive navigation test, the games tester aims to ensure that players can easily navigate through the game's menus and controls. This evaluation helps identify and address issues such as unclear instructions, missing or incorrect icons, and problems with button mapping, providing a more user-friendly and intuitive UI experience for players of "Adventure Legends."

Usability Testing

Usability testing involves testing the game's user interface to ensure that it is easy to use and that players can understand how to play the game. Games testers should check for issues such as confusing tutorials, unclear instructions, and issues with game mechanics.

Game: "Mystic Quest"

Objective: To evaluate the usability of the game's user interface (UI), ensuring that it is easy to use and that players can understand how to play the game. The focus is on testing for issues such as confusing tutorials, unclear instructions, and problems with game mechanics.

==== **Test Scenario** ====
1. Tutorial Evaluation
- The games tester will thoroughly assess the tutorial provided within the game.

- They will evaluate if the tutorial effectively guides players through the game mechanics and provides clear instructions.

- The tester will identify any areas where the tutorial may be confusing or lacking in clarity, ensuring that players can understand how to play the game.

2. Instructions and On-Screen Prompts
- During gameplay, the tester will examine the instructions and on-screen prompts that appear throughout the game.

- They will check for clarity and conciseness, ensuring that players can easily understand what actions to take and how to proceed.

- The tester will identify any instances where instructions or prompts may be unclear or misleading, providing feedback for improvements.

3. Game Mechanics and Controls
- The tester will focus on testing the game mechanics

and controls within the UI.

- They will evaluate if the mechanics are intuitive and easily understood by players.

- The tester will identify any issues with controls, such as unresponsive inputs or unintuitive button mapping, ensuring smooth gameplay.

4. Progression and Goal Clarity

- The tester will assess the clarity of game progression and player goals within the UI.

- They will evaluate if players can easily understand their objectives and track their progress.

- The tester will identify any areas where goals or objectives may be unclear, providing feedback for improved player guidance.

5. Feedback and Response

- The tester will pay attention to the feedback and response provided by the UI during gameplay.

- They will evaluate if the game provides timely and informative feedback to players' actions.

- The tester will identify any areas where feedback may be lacking or confusing, ensuring players receive clear indications of their actions' consequences.

6. Usability and Accessibility

- Throughout the usability test, the tester will consider the overall usability and accessibility of the UI.

- They will assess factors such as font size, colour contrast, and the use of visual cues or indicators to aid understanding and gameplay.

- The tester will provide feedback on any areas where the

UI could be improved to enhance user experience and accommodate diverse player needs.

By conducting a comprehensive usability test, the games tester aims to ensure that the game's UI is user-friendly, allowing players to easily understand how to play the game.

This evaluation helps identify and address issues such as confusing tutorials, unclear instructions, and problems with game mechanics, ultimately providing a more enjoyable and accessible gaming experience for players of "Mystic Quest."

Visual Testing

Visual testing focuses on examining the game's user interface (UI) to guarantee its visual appeal and ensure players can effortlessly access necessary information. Games testers need to be vigilant for potential issues like improper font sizes, colour contrast problems, and any layout or design inconsistencies that might arise.

An example of visual testing being carried out in relation to the user interface is:

Game: "Pixel Adventure"

Objective: To evaluate the usability of the game's visual elements, ensuring that they are visually appealing and easy to comprehend. The focus is on testing for issues such as improper font sizes, color contrast problems, and any layout or design inconsistencies that might arise.

==== Test Scenario ====

1. Font Size Evaluation

- The games tester will thoroughly examine the game's UI to assess the font sizes used throughout.

- They will check if the font sizes are appropriate, ensuring that players can easily read and understand the displayed text.

- The tester will identify any instances of improper font sizes that might hinder readability or cause visual strain.

2. Colour Contrast Analysis

- During gameplay, the tester will evaluate the colour contrast employed within the UI and game elements.

- They will assess if the colours used provide sufficient contrast, making it easy for players to distinguish between different UI elements and important information.

- The tester will identify any areas where colour contrast is lacking, potentially causing visual confusion or making it difficult to read text or interpret visual cues.

3. Layout and Design Consistency

- The tester will focus on examining the overall layout and design consistency within the game's UI.

- They will assess if the UI elements are consistently arranged and follow a coherent design pattern.

- The tester will identify any layout or design inconsistencies that might affect the overall visual appeal or cause confusion for players.

4. Readability of Text

- The tester will pay particular attention to the readability of text displayed within the game.

- They will evaluate if the chosen fonts and text formatting enhance readability, ensuring that players can easily understand the information presented.

- The tester will identify any instances where the text is difficult to read or where formatting choices hinder comprehension.

5. Visual Hierarchy

- The tester will assess the visual hierarchy employed within the UI.

- They will evaluate if important information, such as menu options or gameplay elements, stands out and draws attention appropriately.

- The tester will identify any areas where the visual hierarchy may be unclear or inconsistent, potentially causing confusion for players.

6. Usability and Accessibility

- Throughout the usability test, the tester will consider the overall usability and accessibility of the visual elements within the game.

- They will assess factors such as font size, colour contrast, and layout to ensure they accommodate diverse player needs and provide an enjoyable experience.

- The tester will provide feedback on any areas where improvements can be made to enhance the visual appeal and usability of the game.

By conducting a comprehensive usability test with a focus on visual elements, the games tester aims to ensure that the game's UI is visually appealing, readable, and consistent. This evaluation helps identify and address issues such as improper font sizes, colour contrast problems, and layout or design inconsistencies, ultimately providing a visually engaging and user-friendly experience for players of "Pixel Adventure."

Functionality Testing

Functionality testing involves testing the game's user interface to ensure that it works correctly and that players can navigate the game without encountering any issues. Games testers should check for issues such as button responsiveness, controller compatibility, and input lag.

Game: "Galactic Warriors"

Objective: To evaluate the usability and functionality of the game, ensuring that it performs as intended and provides a smooth gaming experience. The focus is on testing for issues such as button responsiveness, controller compatibility, and input lag.

=== **Test Scenario** ====

1. Button Responsiveness

- The games tester will thoroughly test the responsiveness of various in-game buttons and controls.

- They will assess if the buttons react promptly and accurately to player inputs.

- The tester will identify any instances where buttons are unresponsive or have a delayed response, providing feedback for improvement.

2. Controller Compatibility

- During gameplay, the tester will evaluate the compatibility of different controllers with the game.

- They will test the functionality of popular controllers, ensuring they work seamlessly with the game's controls.

- The tester will identify any compatibility issues or controller mapping inconsistencies that may hinder players from using their preferred controllers effectively.

3. Input Lag Assessment

- The tester will focus on evaluating the input lag within

the game.

- They will assess if there is any noticeable delay between player inputs and the corresponding actions in the game.

- The tester will identify any instances of significant input lag that might affect gameplay responsiveness, providing feedback for optimization.

4. Gameplay Flow

- The tester will evaluate the overall flow of gameplay and interactions with the game's mechanics.

- They will assess if the game mechanics and actions align with the player's expectations, providing a smooth and intuitive gaming experience.

- The tester will identify any areas where gameplay flow may feel clunky or counter-intuitive, suggesting improvements to enhance the overall functionality.

5. Error Handling

- The tester will pay attention to how the game handles errors or unexpected situations.

- They will evaluate if error messages are clear and provide helpful guidance to players.

- The tester will identify any instances where error handling could be improved to minimize confusion or frustration for players.

6. Usability and Accessibility

- Throughout the usability test, the tester will consider the overall usability and accessibility of the game's functionality.

- They will assess factors such as button layout, control scheme options, and input methods to ensure they accommodate diverse player needs.

- The tester will provide feedback on any areas where functionality can be improved to enhance the gaming experience and make it accessible to a wider audience.

By conducting a comprehensive usability test with a focus on functionality, the games tester aims to ensure that the game's buttons are responsive, controller compatibility is smooth, and input lag is minimized.

This evaluation helps identify and address issues that may affect gameplay experience, providing a more enjoyable and user-friendly gaming experience for players of "Galactic Warriors."

Accessibility Testing

Accessibility testing involves testing the game's user interface to ensure that it is accessible to players with disabilities. Games testers should check for issues such as issues with screen readers, font sizes that are too small, and issues with colour contrast.

Example of an accessibility test ran on a game:

Game: "Inclusive Adventures"

Objective: To evaluate the usability and accessibility of the game, ensuring that it can be enjoyed by players of all abilities. The focus is on testing for issues such as screen reader compatibility, font sizes that are too small, and problems with color contrast.

==== Test Scenario ====
1. Screen Reader Compatibility

- The games tester will thoroughly test the game's compatibility with screen readers, software used by visually impaired players.

- They will assess if the game's UI and text elements are properly read by screen readers, providing necessary information to visually impaired players.

- The tester will identify any issues where the game's content is not properly conveyed or where screen reader compatibility is lacking.

2. Font Size and Readability

- During gameplay, the tester will evaluate the font sizes used throughout the game's UI and text elements.

- They will assess if the font sizes are large enough and easily readable, especially for players with visual impairments.

- The tester will identify any instances where the font sizes are too small or difficult to read, providing feedback for increasing readability.

3. Colour Contrast Assessment

- The tester will focus on evaluating the colour contrast used within the game's UI and visual elements.

- They will assess if the colour combinations used provide sufficient contrast, making it easier for players with visual impairments to distinguish between different UI elements and important information.

- The tester will identify any areas where colour contrast is lacking, potentially causing difficulties for players with visual impairments.

4. Alternative Text and Descriptions

- The tester will assess if the game provides alternative text or descriptions for visual elements, ensuring that players with visual impairments can understand the content.

- They will evaluate if images, icons, and visual cues are accompanied by descriptive text or audio cues.

- The tester will identify any instances where alternative text or descriptions are missing or inadequate, providing feedback for improving accessibility.

5.Keyboard and Controller Accessibility

- The tester will evaluate the accessibility of the game's controls, both for keyboard and controller inputs.

- They will assess if players can navigate and interact with the game using alternative input methods, accommodating players with physical disabilities.

- The tester will identify any issues where certain controls or actions may be difficult or impossible for players with mobility limitations.

6. Enhancing Usability for All Players

- Throughout the accessibility test, the tester will keep in mind the importance of making the game usable for players of all abilities.

- They will consider the needs of players with visual impairments, ensuring font sizes are readable and colour contrast is sufficient.

- The tester will also evaluate the game's compatibility with alternative input methods for players with mobility limitations.

Their feedback will focus on improving accessibility features and enhancing the overall gaming experience for everyone.

By conducting a comprehensive usability test with a focus on accessibility, the games tester aims to make "Inclusive Adventures" a game that can be enjoyed by players of all abilities.

This evaluation helps identify and address issues such as screen reader compatibility, font sizes that are too small, and problems with colour contrast. The goal is to create an inclusive and delightful gaming experience, where all players can embark on exciting adventures together.

Games need to meet certain standards for top-rated accessibility testing. The standards may vary based on the platform, but there are some general guidelines that game developers and testers can follow to ensure their games are accessible to all players.

Some of the common standards for accessibility testing include:

Accessibility guidelines: Game developers and testers should follow the accessibility guidelines provided by the platform they are developing the game for, such as Xbox Accessibility Guidelines, PlayStation Accessibility Guidelines, or Nintendo Accessibility Guidelines.

Input methods: Games should allow for multiple input methods, such as keyboard, mouse, joystick, or game pad. They should also provide customizable controls to allow players to adjust the input methods to their preferences.

Visual elements: Games should provide visual elements that are easy to see and distinguish, with clear and legible text, high contrast, and colour-blind friendly options.

Audio Elements: Games should include thoughtful audio features like closed captioning, subtitles, and audio descriptions. These additions ensure that players who are deaf, hard of hearing, or visually impaired can fully immerse themselves in the game world and enjoy the storytelling.

Navigation and Menus: Games should strive for user-friendly navigation and menus, making them easy to navigate and comprehend. Providing clear instructions and intuitive controls ensures that all players can effortlessly explore the game without feeling lost. Additionally, alternative navigation options like voice commands or gesture controls can offer even more accessibility and convenience.

Difficulty levels: Games should offer a range of difficulty levels, ensuring that players of all skill levels and abilities can find the perfect challenge.

By following these accessibility standards, game developers and testers can ensure that their games are accessible to all players, regardless of their abilities.

User interface testing is an essential aspect of video game testing, and games testers must perform it effectively to ensure that the game's user interface is easy to navigate and that players can understand the game's controls and features. Navigation testing, usability testing, visual testing, functionality testing, and accessibility testing are all effective techniques that games testers can use to perform user interface testing.

By performing user interface testing effectively, games testers can help ensure that the game is intuitive and easy to use, regardless of the player's experience level.

Acceptance Testing for
Games Testers

Acceptance testing is a process of testing a video game to ensure that it meets the client's requirements and that it is ready for release. This testing is performed after the game has been developed, and all defects and issues have been resolved. The goal of acceptance testing is to ensure that the game meets the client's expectations and that it is of high quality.

Acceptance Testing Techniques

There are several techniques that games testers can use to perform acceptance testing. These techniques include:

Functionality Testing

Functionality testing involves testing the game's functionality to ensure that it works correctly and that all features and mechanics are working as intended. Games testers should check for issues such as crashes, bugs, and glitches.

Performance Testing

Performance testing involves testing the game's performance to ensure that it meets the client's requirements and that it runs smoothly on all platforms. Games testers should check for issues such as frame rate drops, loading times, and graphics issues.

Regression Testing

Regression testing involves testing the game after changes have been made to ensure that the changes did not introduce new defects or issues. Games testers should check for issues such as broken features, crashes, and bugs.

Localization Testing

Localization testing involves testing the game's localization to ensure that it is accurate and that it meets the client's requirements. Games testers should check for issues such as incorrect translations, incorrect cultural references, and issues with text formatting.

Compliance Testing
Compliance testing involves testing the game to ensure that it meets industry standards and regulations. Games testers should check for issues such as issues with age ratings, licensing requirements, and issues with content.

The types of testing above have already been mentioned several times in the previous sections and with examples. In this instance we will keep it short and concise as some of the testing points overlap with the regression testing in the next section.

Acceptance testing is a critical phase in the video game development process, and games testers must perform it effectively to ensure that the game meets the client's requirements and that it is ready for release. Functionality testing, performance testing, regression testing, localization testing, and compliance testing are all effective techniques that games testers can use to perform acceptance testing.

By performing acceptance testing effectively, games testers can help ensure that the game is of high quality and that it meets the client's expectations.

Regression Testing for Games Testers

Regression testing involves thoroughly examining a video game after updates or changes have been implemented. Its purpose is to verify that these modifications haven't introduced new defects or issues, maintaining the game's stability and functionality.

Techniques for Regression Testing

Games testers employ various techniques to conduct effective regression testing. These techniques include:

Re-testing

Re-testing involves testing the game to ensure that the defects or issues that were identified during the previous testing cycle have been resolved. Games testers should check for issues such as crashes, bugs, and glitches.

An example of a re-test being carried out:

Game: "Galactic Warriors"

Objective: To conduct a regression test on the game to verify that defects or issues identified in the previous testing cycle have been successfully resolved. The focus is on checking for issues such as crashes, bugs, and glitches.

==== Test Scenario ====
Defect Resolution Verification

- The games tester will re-test the areas of the game where defects or issues were previously identified.

- They will execute the same actions and interactions that initially triggered the problems, carefully observing for any recurrence.

- The tester will verify if the reported crashes, bugs, or

glitches have been effectively resolved, ensuring the game's stability.

Crash Testing

- During gameplay, the tester will stress-test the game to identify any potential crashes or unexpected terminations.

- They will perform actions that have previously caused the game to crash or exhibit instability, aiming to uncover any lingering issues.

- The tester will document and report any new instances of crashes, ensuring that they are resolved before the game's release.

Bug and Glitch Verification

- The tester will re-examine areas where bugs or glitches were previously encountered to validate their resolution.

- They will meticulously check for any visual anomalies, incorrect behaviors, or missing features that were previously reported.

- The tester will document and report any instances where the reported bugs or glitches persist, requiring further attention.

Comprehensive Functionality Check

- In addition to re-testing specific defects, the tester will perform a thorough evaluation of the game's overall functionality.

- They will execute various actions, interactions, and game mechanics to ensure all aspects are working as intended.

- The tester will identify any new issues or unexpected

behaviours that may have been introduced during the defect resolution process.

By conducting a comprehensive regression test with a focus on re-testing, the games tester aims to confirm the resolution of previously identified defects or issues.

This evaluation ensures that the game is stable, functional, and free from crashes, bugs, and glitches, offering players a smooth and enjoyable experience in the thrilling universe of "Galactic Warriors."

Smoke Testing

Smoke testing involves testing the game's most critical features to ensure that they still work correctly after changes have been made. Games testers should check for issues such as crashes, game-breaking bugs, and glitches.

An example of performing a smoke test:

Game: "Mystic Quest"

Objective: To conduct a regression test by performing smoke testing on the game's critical features, ensuring they work correctly after recent changes. The focus is on checking for issues such as crashes, game-breaking bugs, and glitches.

==== Test Scenario ====
Critical Feature Validation

- The games tester will prioritize testing the game's most critical features that have undergone recent changes.

- They will focus on executing key actions and interactions necessary for the smooth progression of gameplay.

- The tester will carefully observe for any issues such as crashes, game-breaking bugs, or glitches that may disrupt the critical features.

Crash Testing

- During gameplay, the tester will stress-test the critical features to identify any potential crashes or unexpected terminations.

- They will perform actions that previously caused the game to crash, aiming to uncover any persisting instability.

- The tester will document and report any new instances of crashes, ensuring that they are addressed promptly.

Game-Breaking Bug Identification

- The tester will actively search for any game-breaking bugs that may hinder progress or render the game unplayable.

- They will execute critical actions and sequences to identify any issues that impede the intended gameplay experience.

- The tester will document and report any newly discovered game-breaking bugs, providing detailed information for their resolution.

Glitch Detection

- Throughout the regression test, the tester will keep an eye out for glitches or graphical anomalies in the critical features.

- They will examine visual elements, animations, and interactions to identify any abnormalities or visual distortions.

- The tester will document any glitches observed, ensuring they are addressed to maintain a polished gaming experience.

By conducting thorough regression testing with a focus on

smoke testing, the games tester aims to validate the correct functionality of critical features after recent changes. This evaluation ensures that the game remains stable, free from crashes, game-breaking bugs, and glitches, offering players a seamless and immersive experience in the captivating world of "Mystic Quest."

Test Case Prioritization

Test case prioritization involves prioritizing the test cases based on their importance and impact on the game. This technique ensures that the most critical test cases are tested first and that the game's most critical features are tested thoroughly.

Example of test case prioritization during testing:

Game: "Epic Quest"

Objective: To prioritize test cases during the development phase of the game, ensuring efficient allocation of testing efforts and resources.

==== Test Scenario ====
User Interface (UI) Testing

- Test cases related to UI elements, such as menus, buttons, and navigation, are prioritized to ensure a seamless user experience.

- This includes verifying the correct placement, appearance, and functionality of UI components.

- UI test cases take precedence as they directly impact the players' interaction with the game.

Gameplay Mechanics

- Test cases focusing on core gameplay mechanics and interactions are given high priority.

- These include testing player movements, combat mechanics, item interactions, and character abilities.

- Ensuring that the game mechanics function as intended is crucial for providing an engaging and enjoyable gaming experience.

Game Progression and Quests

- Test cases related to game progression, quests, and missions are prioritized to ensure a smooth and logical flow throughout the game.

- This includes verifying that quests can be completed, objectives are clear, and progression is not hindered by any blockers or glitches.

- Testing game progression is essential as it directly impacts the players' ability to advance and experience the game's narrative.

Stability and Performance

- Test cases focusing on the stability and performance of the game, such as memory usage, loading times, and overall responsiveness, are prioritized.

- Ensuring that the game runs smoothly without crashes, freezes, or significant performance issues is crucial for a satisfying gameplay experience.

Multiplayer Functionality

- If the game includes multiplayer features, test cases related to multiplayer functionality are given priority.

- This includes testing matchmaking, network connectivity, player interactions, and synchronization between players.

- Verifying the stability and seamless operation of multiplayer features is essential for a successful multiplayer experience.

By prioritizing test cases during the development phase of

"Epic Quest," the games tester can ensure that the most critical aspects of the game are thoroughly tested first. This approach allows for efficient allocation of testing efforts and resources, focusing on areas that have the greatest impact on user experience and overall game quality.

Automated Testing

Automated testing involves using automated tools to test the game's functionality after changes have been made. This technique saves time and effort and ensures that the game is tested thoroughly.

Example of automated testing:

Game: "Virtual Racer"

Objective: To test the game "Virtual Racer" using an automated testing process to increase efficiency and coverage.

==== Test Scenario ====
Test Case Selection
- The games tester selects a set of test cases that cover various aspects of the game, such as gameplay mechanics, UI, and performance.

- These test cases are converted into automated scripts or test scenarios, ready to be executed by the automated testing tools.

Test Environment Setup
- The tester sets up the test environment, including the game installation, required hardware and software configurations, and any necessary testing tools.

- They ensure that the automated testing framework is properly integrated with the game to execute the automated test scripts effectively.

Test Script Execution
- The automated testing tools execute the prepared test

scripts or scenarios, emulating user interactions and actions within the game.

- These tools simulate inputs, such as button presses, mouse movements, and keystrokes, following the predefined test scripts.

Test Result Analysis
- The automated testing tools collect data and log the test results, capturing any deviations or issues encountered during the test execution.

- The tester analyses the test reports generated by the automated tools, identifying any failures, errors, or unexpected behaviours.

Issue Reporting and Bug Tracking
- Whenever the automated testing process detects a problem or unexpected behaviour, the tester reports it to the development team in a friendly and informative manner.

- The tester includes all relevant details, such as clear descriptions, screenshots, and steps to reproduce the issue, to help the developers understand and address the problem effectively.

Test Maintenance and Enhancement
- As the game evolves and improves, the tester takes care of keeping the automated test scripts up-to-date and accurate.

- They work closely with the development team, updating the test scripts to match any changes in features or mechanics, ensuring that the testing remains thorough and comprehensive.

- By maintaining and enhancing the test scripts, the tester contributes to the ongoing success of the automated testing process, helping to deliver a top-notch gaming experience to the players.

By utilizing an automated testing process, the games tester can significantly increase the efficiency and coverage of testing for "Virtual Racer." This approach reduces the manual effort required, allowing for faster and more consistent testing across multiple test cases.

Regression testing is a critical phase in the video game testing process, and games testers must perform it effectively to ensure that the game remains stable and functional after changes have been made. Re-testing, smoke testing, test case prioritization, and automated testing are all effective techniques that games testers can use to perform regression testing.

By performing regression testing effectively, games testers can help ensure that the game is of high quality and that it remains stable and functional after changes have been made.

CHAPTER 5 - TESTING TECHNIQUES AND TOOLS

As video games become more complex, testing them thoroughly becomes increasingly important. In order to ensure that a game is of high quality and functions properly, games testers must use a variety of testing techniques and tools. This chapter will explore some of the most commonly used testing techniques and tools used by games testers, including manual testing, automation testing, load testing, and more.

By understanding and utilizing these techniques and tools, games testers can ensure that the games they test are of the highest quality possible.

Exploratory Testing for
Games Testers

Exploratory testing is a special kind of testing where games testers actively dive into the game to discover any defects or issues that may have slipped past other testing methods. This testing approach is spontaneous and relies on the experience and intuition of the games tester to uncover hidden problems. Exploratory testing teams up wonderfully with other testing techniques, and it can be flexibly performed at any stage of the testing process.

Imagine this: armed with a sense of adventure and a deep love for games, testers immerse themselves in the virtual world, leaving no stone unturned. They become the heroes of quality assurance, meticulously exploring every corner, trying out various interactions, and pushing the game's boundaries to expose any lurking surprises. It's like embarking on a grand quest to unveil those elusive bugs and glitches that traditional methods might miss.

What makes exploratory testing truly exciting is its flexibility. Testers can embark on this adventure at any point during the game's development, from its early stages to its final polish. It seamlessly complements other testing techniques, injecting a dose of creativity and adaptability into the quest for quality.

The secret to success lies in collaboration. Games testers work hand in hand with the development team, forming an unstoppable alliance. They share valuable insights, engage in discussions, and provide detailed feedback. Together, they navigate the game's intricacies, ensuring a flawless gaming experience that will captivate players.

Why is Exploratory Testing Important for Games Testers?
Exploratory testing is an important technique for games testers

for several reasons. First, it allows games testers to identify defects or issues that may not have been found through other testing techniques. This is especially important for games that are complex or have a large number of features, as it can be difficult to identify all potential issues through scripted testing alone.

Second, exploratory testing allows games testers to gain a deeper understanding of the game and its mechanics. By exploring the game in an unscripted manner, games testers can identify potential issues that may not have been considered during scripted testing. This can help to improve the overall quality of the game and ensure that it is enjoyable for players.

How to Perform Exploratory Testing Effectively
To perform exploratory testing effectively, games testers should follow a few key steps. First, they should create a list of areas of the game that they want to explore. This list should be based on the tester's experience and intuition, as well as any potential issues that have been identified through scripted testing.

In the unscripted exploration phase, games testers thoroughly investigate every aspect of the game, focusing on mechanics, controls, and overall performance. Their keen eye detects potential issues or defects, which they promptly document with clarity. This includes noting the issue's location, steps to reproduce it, and capturing relevant visuals for reference.

Exploratory testing is an important technique for games testers that allows them to identify potential defects or issues that may not have been found through other testing techniques. By following the steps outlined in this chapter, games testers can perform exploratory testing effectively and improve the overall quality of the games they test.

Boundary Testing for Games Testers

Boundary testing is a type of testing that involves testing the boundaries of the game to identify defects or issues. This testing typically involves testing the upper and lower limits of the game's mechanics, such as maximum and minimum values for health or ammunition. The goal of boundary testing is to identify any issues or defects that may arise when the game is pushed to its limits.

Why is Boundary Testing Important for Games Testers?

Boundary testing is an important technique for games testers for several reasons. First, it allows games testers to identify potential issues or defects that may occur when the game is pushed to its limits. For example, a game may be able to handle a certain number of players at once, but may begin to experience issues if too many players are in the same area.

Second, boundary testing allows games testers to ensure that the game is fair and balanced for all players. By testing the upper and lower limits of the game's mechanics, games testers can ensure that all players have a fair and equal chance to succeed in the game.

How to Perform Boundary Testing Effectively

To perform boundary testing effectively, games testers should follow a few key steps.

First, they should identify the boundaries of the game's mechanics, such as the maximum and minimum values for health or ammunition. Next, games testers should begin testing at the lower boundary of the game's mechanics, such as testing the game with a player character that has the minimum amount of health.

They should then gradually increase the values until they reach the upper boundary, such as testing the game with a player character that has the maximum amount of health. As potential issues or defects are identified, games testers should document them in a clear and concise manner, including information such as the location of the issue, the steps to reproduce it, and any relevant screenshots or video.

Boundary testing is an important technique for games testers that allows them to identify potential issues or defects that may occur when the game is pushed to its limits.

Negative Testing for Games Testers

Negative testing is a type of testing that involves intentionally attempting to break or fail the game by inputting incorrect or unexpected data. This testing typically involves testing the game with invalid or unexpected inputs to see how the game reacts. The goal of negative testing is to identify any issues or defects that may arise when the game encounters unexpected data or situations.

Why is Negative Testing Important for Games Testers?
Negative testing is an important technique for games testers for several reasons. First, it allows games testers to identify potential issues or defects that may occur when the game encounters unexpected data or situations.

For example, a game may crash if it encounters an unexpected combination of inputs from the player. Second, negative testing allows games testers to ensure that the game is secure and protected from potential hacks or exploits. By intentionally attempting to input incorrect or unexpected data, games testers can identify potential security vulnerabilities in the game.

How to Perform Negative Testing Effectively
To perform negative testing effectively, games testers should follow a few key steps. First, they should identify the areas of the game that are most vulnerable to unexpected data or situations.

For example, areas of the game that involve user input, such as character creation or item selection screens, are often vulnerable to unexpected inputs. Next, games testers should attempt to input invalid or unexpected data in these areas of the game, such as attempting to create a character with a name that contains invalid characters or selecting an item that is not available in the game.

As potential issues or defects are identified, games testers should document them in a clear and concise manner, including information such as the location of the issue, input characters used, the steps to reproduce it, and any relevant screenshots or video.

Negative testing is an important technique for games testers that allows them to identify potential issues or defects that may arise when the game encounters unexpected data or situations.

Black-Box Testing for Games Testers

Black box testing holds significance in game testing as it contributes to the assurance of a game's overall quality, functionality, and user experience. This method involves testers evaluating the game from an external standpoint, devoid of any understanding of its internal code or structure.

Why is Black-Box Testing Important for Games Testers?

Black-box testing is an important technique for games testers for several reasons. First, it allows games testers to identify potential issues or defects that may be experienced by typical players. By testing the game without knowledge of its internal code or structure, games testers can more accurately simulate the experience of a typical player and identify issues that may arise during normal gameplay.

Second, black-box testing allows games testers to ensure that the game meets the expectations of typical players. By testing the game as it would be experienced by a typical player, games testers can ensure that the game is intuitive and easy to use, and that it meets the expectations of typical players in terms of gameplay mechanics and difficulty.

How to Perform Black-Box Testing Effectively

In order to conduct black-box testing with proficiency, game testers need to adhere to certain essential steps. Initially, they must adopt the perspective of an ordinary player, devoid of any prior understanding of the game's code or structure. This entails refraining from inspecting the game's code or structure and concentrating solely on testing the game in a manner that aligns with the typical player experience.

Next, games testers should attempt to test all aspects of the game, including gameplay mechanics, user interfaces, graphics, sound, and any other relevant features. By testing all aspects of the game, games testers can ensure that the game is polished and meets the expectations of typical players.

As potential issues or defects are identified, games testers should document them in a clear and concise manner, including information such as the location of the issue, the steps to reproduce it, and any relevant screenshots or video.

Black-box testing stands as a significant approach for games testers, enabling them to pinpoint possible problems or flaws that may arise during the gaming experience of average players. By diligently adhering to the steps outlined in this chapter, games testers can proficiently conduct black-box testing, leading to enhanced quality and user experience in the games they test.

White-Box Testing for Games Testers

For a games tester, white-box testing holds considerable significance as it involves delving into the internal code and structure of a game. Unlike black-box testing, white-box testing provides testers with in-depth knowledge of the game's internal workings. This allows them to explore and evaluate the underlying mechanisms, logic, and algorithms employed within the game.

By conducting white-box testing, games testers can meticulously examine the game's internal components, identify potential issues or flaws, and ensure the desired functionality and quality of the game. It empowers testers to uncover bugs, optimize performance, and contribute to the overall refinement of the game's development process.

What is White-Box Testing?

White-box testing encompasses a form of testing wherein the game is examined with an understanding of its internal code and structure. The primary objective of white-box testing is to scrutinize the internal mechanisms of the game and verify their intended functionality. Typically, developers undertake white-box testing, although games testers equipped with knowledge of the game's code and structure can also perform this type of testing.

Why is White-Box Testing Important for Games Testers?

White-box testing is an important technique for games testers for several reasons. First, it allows games testers to identify potential issues or defects that may be related to the game's internal code or structure. By testing the game with knowledge of its internal workings, games testers can identify issues that may not be visible during black-box testing.

Second, white-box testing allows games testers to ensure that the game is optimized for performance. By testing the game's internal code and structure, games testers can identify potential performance bottlenecks and work with developers to optimize the game's performance.

How to Perform White-Box Testing Effectively

To perform white-box testing effectively, games testers should follow a few key steps. First, they should have knowledge of the game's internal code and structure. This may require working closely with developers or obtaining documentation on the game's code and structure.

Next, games testers should attempt to test all aspects of the game's internal workings, including code, algorithms, and data structures. By testing all aspects of the game's internal workings, games testers can identify potential issues or defects and work with developers to address them.

As potential issues or defects are identified, games testers should document them in a clear and concise manner, including information such as the location of the issue, the steps to reproduce it, and any relevant code snippets.

White-box testing is an important technique for games testers that allows them to identify potential issues or defects related to the game's internal code and structure. By following the steps outlined in this chapter, games testers can perform white-box testing effectively and improve the overall quality and performance of the games they test.

Test Automation Tools
for Games Testers

In the realm of games testing, test automation involves the utilization of software tools to orchestrate test executions and compare the attained outcomes against the anticipated results. This chapter delves into the fundamentals of test automation tools, emphasizing their significance for games testers and providing insights into their effective utilization.

By delving into this subject, games testers can gain a comprehensive understanding of test automation tools and harness their potential to enhance testing efficiency and accuracy.

What are Test Automation Tools?
Test automation tools are software programs that are used to automate the testing process. These tools can automate a wide range of testing tasks, from simple tasks like generating test data to more complex tasks like simulating user interactions.

Why are Test Automation Tools Important for Games Testers?
Test automation tools hold immense value for games testers due to multiple reasons. Primarily, they serve as time-saving and efficiency-enhancing aids. By automating repetitive testing tasks, games testers can allocate their time and effort towards more intricate and crucial testing endeavours.

This allows them to prioritize complex scenarios, thoroughly examine critical aspects of the game, and dedicate their expertise to uncovering potential issues and optimizing the overall testing process. As a result, test automation tools prove indispensable in streamlining testing efforts and maximizing the productivity of games testers.

Secondly, test automation tools can help games testers improve the accuracy and consistency of their testing. Automation tools can execute tests faster and more accurately than manual testing, and can help games testers identify issues more quickly.

Third, test automation tools can help games testers test their games across a wide range of devices and platforms. By using automation tools to run tests on different devices and platforms, games testers can identify issues and ensure that their games are compatible with a wide range of systems.

How to Use Test Automation Tools Effectively
To use test automation tools effectively, games testers should follow a few key steps. First, they should identify which tests are good candidates for automation. Tests that are repetitive, time-consuming, or require large amounts of data are good candidates for automation.

Next, games testers should select the right automation tool for their needs. There are many test automation tools available, ranging from free open-source tools to commercial tools with advanced features. Games testers should evaluate their needs and budget and choose a tool that best fits their requirements.

Once a tool has been selected, games testers should create a test automation plan. This plan should identify which tests will be automated, the expected results, and the steps required to execute the tests. Games testers should also ensure that their test automation scripts are maintainable and reusable.

Games testers commonly employ various test automation tools, some of which include:

Unity Test Runner: As an integrated testing framework within the Unity game engine, it enables the automation of tests specifically for Unity-based games.

Appium: This open-source tool specializes in automating tests for mobile games, accommodating both Android and iOS platforms.

Selenium: This widely used open-source tool focuses on automating tests for web-based games, facilitating user interaction simulation and issue identification.

Cucumber: Offering a behaviour driven development (BDD) style, this tool allows testers to write and automate tests in a more readable and understandable manner.

TestComplete: As a commercial testing tool, it enables testers to automate tests for desktop and mobile games, supporting diverse platforms and devices.

JMeter: This open-source tool serves the purpose of performance testing in games, simulating heavy user loads and uncovering performance bottlenecks.

These examples highlight a range of test automation tools available to games testers. Evaluating their specific requirements and criteria is essential in selecting the most suitable tool for their testing needs.

Performance testing tools

The significance of test automation tools for games testers lies in their potential to enhance efficiency, precision, and consistency. By adhering to the guidelines presented in this chapter, games testers can effectively leverage test automation tools to elevate the quality of the games they test and ensure compatibility across a diverse array of devices and platforms.

Within game testing, performance testing stands as a crucial element, aiming to identify and rectify issues pertaining to performance, such as lag, slow load times, and low frame rates. To carry out performance testing, game testers have access to a range of specialized tools tailored explicitly for games. This chapter delves into an exploration of some of the most prominent performance testing tools available to game testers, shedding light on their features, functionalities, and benefits.

Unity Performance Testing: Unity is a popular game engine that comes with a built-in performance testing framework. This framework allows game testers to create test cases that simulate heavy loads and measure the performance of the game in real-time. Testers can use this tool to identify bottlenecks and optimize the performance of the game.

GameBench: GameBench is a commercial tool that is designed specifically for mobile game testing. It allows testers to measure the performance of mobile games on different devices and platforms. Testers can use this tool to identify performance issues and optimize the game for better performance.

Intel Graphics Performance Analyzers (Intel GPA): Intel GPA is a free tool that is designed for performance analysis of games. It can be used to analyze the graphics performance of the game and identify bottlenecks that affect the game's performance. It provides real-time metrics and can be used to optimize the game for better performance.

NVIDIA Nsight: NVIDIA Nsight is a commercial tool that is designed for performance analysis of games. It can be used to analyze the graphics performance of the game on NVIDIA GPUs and identify bottlenecks that affect the game's performance. It provides real-time metrics and can be used to optimize the game for better performance.

Fraps: Fraps is a popular tool that can be used to measure the frame rate of games. It provides real-time metrics on the frame rate and can be used to identify performance issues such as low frame rates and stuttering.

Performance Monitor: Performance Monitor is a built-in tool in Windows that can be used to monitor the performance of games. It provides real-time metrics on the CPU, GPU, and memory usage of the game. Testers can use this tool to identify bottlenecks and optimize the game for better performance.

In conclusion, performance testing is crucial for ensuring that games run smoothly and provide the best possible user experience. Game testers can use a variety of performance testing tools to measure the performance of games and identify performance issues. By using these tools, game testers can optimize the performance of games and provide a better gaming experience for users.

Debugging Tools for Game Testers

Debugging is an essential part of the game development process that ensures the game's stability and functionality. Game testers use various debugging tools to identify and fix bugs, errors, and glitches in the game. Debugging tools can be divided into two categories: in-game debugging tools and external debugging tools.

In-Game Debugging Tools

In-game debugging tools are built-in features of the game that allow testers to view the game's internal state in real-time. These tools enable testers to monitor game variables, track player movements, view the game's performance metrics, and analyse the game's behaviour under different conditions. In-game debugging tools are specific to each game engine and can vary depending on the game developer's preferences.

Unity3D, a popular game engine, provides a range of in-game debugging tools, including the Unity Profiler, which measures the game's performance and provides detailed reports on frame rate, memory usage, and CPU usage. The Unity Editor also features a Console window that displays error messages and warnings, which help testers identify and fix issues in the game's code.

Unreal Engine, another widely-used game engine, provides a comprehensive set of debugging tools, including the Unreal Editor, which allows testers to view and modify game assets, and the Unreal Console, which displays real-time information about the game's performance and behaviour.

External Debugging Tools

External debugging tools are third-party software tools that are used to monitor and analyse the game's behaviour outside of the game's engine. These tools provide a more in-depth view of the game's internal state, including the game's memory usage, network traffic, and system resources. External debugging tools can be used in combination with in-game debugging tools to provide a more comprehensive view of the game's performance.

One example of an external debugging tool is Visual Studio Debugger, which provides a range of debugging features, including real-time code analysis, breakpoints, and memory monitoring. Testers can use Visual Studio Debugger to track down and fix bugs in the game's code.

Another useful external debugging tool is the Microsoft Windows Performance Toolkit, which provides a set of performance analysis tools for Windows-based systems. These tools allow testers to monitor the game's CPU usage, memory usage, disk activity, and network traffic.

Debugging plays a vital role in game testing, and the utilization of appropriate debugging tools can greatly enhance the efficiency and precision of the testing endeavour. In-game debugging tools furnish testers with real-time insights into the game's performance and behaviour, whereas external debugging tools offer a more comprehensive understanding of the game's internal state.

Through a strategic amalgamation of in-game and external debugging tools, testers can swiftly identify and address bugs, guaranteeing a stable, functional, and enjoyable game experience for players. This integrated approach expedites the debugging process, contributing to the overall quality and seamless gameplay of the game.

CHAPTER 6 - PLANNING AND EXECUTING VIDEO GAME TESTS

For games testers, possessing a comprehensive grasp of efficient test planning and execution is paramount. This process holds immense significance in guaranteeing a game's quality, functionality, and ability to meet player expectations. This chapter serves as a guide, shedding light on the diverse stages encompassing test planning and execution for video games.

Moreover, it delves into invaluable best practices aimed at streamlining the testing procedure, minimizing errors, and ultimately enhancing the overall quality of the game. By embracing these insights, games testers can optimize their testing efforts and contribute to the creation of exceptional gaming experiences.

The creation of a test plan stands as a crucial stage in the meticulous testing of a game, aiming to identify and resolve any issues prior to its release. Serving as a comprehensive roadmap, a test plan outlines the testing process, the objectives to be achieved, the necessary resources, and the associated timelines.

Define the Objectives: The first step in creating a test plan is to define the objectives of the tests. This includes identifying the different types of tests required, such as functional testing, compatibility testing, performance testing, etc. It is also important to define the scope of the tests and identify any specific features or functionality that require testing.

Identify the Testing Approach: Once the objectives have been defined, the next step is to identify the testing approach that will be used. This includes determining the testing methods that will be employed, such as manual testing, automated testing, or a combination of both. It is also important to identify the tools and technologies that will be used to carry out the testing.

Determine the Resources Required: The next step is to determine the resources required for the testing process. This includes identifying the team members who will be responsible for carrying out the tests, as well as any external resources required, such as testing tools, equipment, or software.

Define the Test Cases: Once the objectives, testing approach, and resources have been identified, the next step is to define the test cases. Test cases are essentially a set of instructions that outline the steps to be taken to carry out the tests. Each test case should be well-defined and should include a clear set of steps to be taken, the expected results, and any relevant notes or observations.

Set Timelines and Milestones: It is important to set timelines and milestones for the testing process to ensure that the tests are carried out in a timely and efficient manner. This includes identifying specific deadlines for completing different stages of the testing process, as well as defining milestones for measuring progress.

Identify Risks and Contingencies: Finally, it is important to identify any risks or contingencies that may arise during the testing process. This includes identifying potential issues that may impact the testing process, such as resource constraints, schedule delays, or technical challenges. It is also important to identify contingency plans for addressing these issues if they arise.

Creating a comprehensive test plan is a critical step in ensuring the quality and functionality of a video game. By following these key steps, games testers can create an effective test plan that ensures that the game is thoroughly tested and any issues are identified and addressed before release.

Test Case Design for Games Testers

Designing test cases holds paramount importance in the realm of software testing, including the specialized domain of video game testing. Test cases are meticulously crafted to encompass various facets of the game, such as functionality, performance, usability, compatibility, and localization.

A thoughtfully designed test case serves as a powerful tool for defect identification and plays a vital role in ensuring that the game adheres to the desired quality standards. Within this chapter, we delve into the significance of test case design specifically for games testers, shedding light on the process of constructing highly effective test cases.

The Importance of Test Case Design for Games Testers

The significance of test case design in the realm of games testing cannot be overstated. It plays a pivotal role in defect identification and guarantees that the game meets the necessary quality benchmarks. A meticulously constructed test case empowers testers to meticulously evaluate all aspects and functionalities of the game, leaving no critical features untested.

Additionally, test cases assist in pinpointing potential weaknesses, such as compatibility issues or performance concerns, thereby providing valuable insights for optimization. By focusing on thorough test case design, games testers can enhance their ability to ensure a high-quality, robust gaming experience.

Furthermore, effective test case design helps testers prioritize their testing efforts. Games testers must test a large number of features and aspects of a game, but it is not always possible to test everything. Test case design helps testers focus on critical areas and prioritize testing efforts, ensuring that the most critical aspects of the game are tested thoroughly.

The Process of Creating
Effective Test Cases

Creating effective test cases requires a structured approach. The following steps are typically involved in the process of creating effective test cases for games testers:

Understand the game requirements: Test case design starts with an understanding of the game requirements. Games testers should review the game requirements to understand what features the game should have and what standards it should meet. This understanding will guide the tester in creating relevant test cases.

Identify the test scenarios: Once the game requirements are understood, games testers should identify the test scenarios that need to be tested. Test scenarios describe the expected behaviour of the game under different conditions. For example, a test scenario for a racing game may include testing the game's performance under different weather conditions.

Create test cases: The process of creating test cases commences with the identification of relevant test scenarios. These scenarios serve as the foundation upon which test cases are built. Test cases provide a detailed description of the specific steps that must be executed to thoroughly test a particular scenario. For instance, in the context of a racing game, a test case might entail evaluating the car's speed and performance in varying weather conditions.

This would involve systematically assessing factors such as acceleration, handling, and traction under different weather scenarios, such as rain, snow, or sunshine. By precisely outlining the steps to be followed, test cases enable games testers to conduct thorough and targeted evaluations, ensuring that the game functions optimally across a diverse range of scenarios.

Define the test data: Test data is the input that is required for a test case to be executed. Testers should define the test data required for each test case. This data can include user names, passwords, game settings, and other parameters.

Prioritize the test cases: Once the test cases are created, games testers should prioritize them based on criticality. Critical test cases should be tested first, followed by less critical test cases.

Execute the test cases: After prioritizing the test cases, games testers should execute them. During execution, testers should record the results of each test case, including any defects found.

Update the test cases: Test cases should be updated if any issues are identified during testing. This ensures that the test cases remain relevant and effective.

Test case design is a crucial activity for games testers. It helps testers identify defects, prioritize testing efforts, and ensure that the game meets the required quality standards. The process of creating effective test cases involves understanding the game requirements, identifying test scenarios, creating test cases, defining test data, prioritizing test cases, executing test cases, and updating test cases. By following these steps, games testers can create effective test cases that ensure the game meets the desired quality standards.

Test Environment Setup

Test environment setup is a critical aspect of the testing process for games testers. The test environment is the system configuration, software, and hardware required to execute test cases and evaluate the game's performance. The setup must reflect the game's deployment environment, which may vary depending on the platform or device the game is intended for. As such, it is essential to establish a comprehensive test environment that mimics the end-users' actual environment. A well-defined test environment setup can help testers identify issues early on in the development process and avoid expensive fixes in later stages.

The first step in setting up a test environment is to identify the hardware and software required for testing. Testers should consider factors such as operating systems, processors, graphics cards, and memory requirements when selecting the hardware. For software, testers must determine the version of the game, as well as any additional software required for testing, such as drivers or plug-ins.

Once the hardware and software requirements are identified, testers can begin setting up the test environment. This typically involves installing the necessary software and drivers, configuring the hardware, and ensuring that all the components are functioning correctly. For example, if the game is being developed for multiple platforms, testers will need to set up each platform's test environment to ensure comprehensive testing.
After the test environment is set up, testers should validate the setup to ensure that it is functioning correctly. This involves executing test cases and ensuring that the game performs as expected. Any issues with the setup must be identified and resolved before testing begins.

Test environment setup is an ongoing process, and testers must maintain the setup as the game evolves. Changes in the game, such as new features or platforms, may require modifications to the test environment. Additionally, the test environment should be kept up to date with the latest versions of the software and hardware components to ensure accurate results.

A well-designed test environment setup is critical for game testers to perform comprehensive testing and identify issues early on in the development process. Testers must identify the hardware and software requirements, configure the test environment, validate the setup, and maintain it throughout the testing process. Proper test environment setup can improve the game's quality, reduce the cost of development, and ensure that the end-users have an enjoyable gaming experience.

Test execution and tracking are critical components of the game testing process. It involves the actual running of the tests, tracking defects, and reporting the results. As a game tester, it is essential to understand the process of test execution and tracking to ensure that the game is thoroughly tested and any issues are resolved before the game is released.

Test Execution
The test execution process involves running the test cases developed in the previous phase. During test execution, the tester ensures that the game is functioning as intended and that all the requirements are being met. The tester must execute the tests on various platforms, such as desktop computers, consoles, and mobile devices, to ensure that the game runs smoothly on all the intended platforms.

Test Tracking
Test tracking involves identifying, logging, and tracking defects found during testing. A defect is any deviation from the expected behavior of the game. It is essential to document defects clearly and accurately, including steps to reproduce the issue and the severity level. The tester should also include

screenshots or videos of the defect, making it easier for the development team to understand and fix the problem.

Test Reporting

Test reporting involves communicating the results of the testing process to the development team. The report should include the number of defects found, their severity level, and the steps taken to reproduce the issues. The tester should also provide a summary of the testing process and the results, including any recommendations or concerns.

As a game tester, it is essential to use a tracking tool to record and report the testing results accurately. The tracking tool can help manage the testing process, including the status of the tests, the severity level of the defects, and the development team's progress in fixing the issues.

In conclusion, test execution and tracking are critical parts of the game testing process. A game tester must execute the tests on various platforms, track defects accurately, and report the results clearly to the development team. By doing so, the game will be thoroughly tested, and any issues will be resolved before the game's release, ensuring the game's success.

Reporting and Documenting

Reporting and documenting bugs is a crucial aspect of game testing, as it enables developers to address and fix issues before release. Game testers must have the skills to clearly and accurately report bugs to developers, as well as track their progress to ensure they are resolved in a timely manner.

When a bug is found, the tester should document the issue with as much detail as possible. This should include the steps taken to reproduce the issue, any error messages received, and any relevant screenshots or videos. The tester should also note the severity of the bug and its impact on gameplay.

Once a bug is documented, it should be reported to the

development team through a bug tracking system or software. This allows the team to prioritize and assign the bug to the appropriate developer for resolution. It is important for the tester to track the progress of the bug, following up with the developer to ensure it is being addressed.

In addition to reporting and tracking bugs, game testers must also document their testing process and findings. This includes creating test reports that detail the tests performed, the results obtained, and any bugs or issues encountered. This documentation is important for future reference and can also help developers identify areas for improvement in the game.

Effective reporting and documentation require strong communication skills and meticulous attention to detail. Game testers must clearly express their observations and provide precise documentation, enabling efficient issue resolution. Moreover, they should collaborate adeptly with developers and team members to accurately track and address bugs.

CHAPTER 7 – WORKING PRACTISES IN GAME DEVELOPMENT TEAMS

Games testers can work within various work practices, including Agile, Waterfall, and other models. The choice of work practice often depends on the development methodology adopted by the game development team or company. Here are some commonly used models:

Agile: Agile methodologies, such as Scrum or Kanban, are increasingly popular in the game development industry. Games testers working in an Agile environment collaborate closely with developers, frequently test small iterations or features, and provide feedback throughout the development process. This iterative approach allows for flexibility and faster adaptation to changes.

What is Agile?
Agile methodology is a project management and software development approach that focuses on adaptability, collaboration, and continuous improvement. It emerged as a response to the rigid waterfall model, which follows a linear and

sequential process.

In agile methodology, projects are divided into shorter iterations known as "sprints." These sprints, lasting a few weeks, involve the development, testing, and implementation of specific features or deliverables. The key principles of agile methodology are as follows:

Customer collaboration takes precedence over negotiating contracts: Agile methodology prioritizes continuous collaboration with customers and stakeholders to ensure their evolving needs are met. Regular feedback and active involvement of stakeholders are central to the agile approach.

Embracing change over rigid planning: Agile teams readily adapt to changes in requirements and priorities, recognizing that they can shift throughout the development process. They are quick to adjust project scope and priorities in response to changing circumstances.

Delivering working software over extensive documentation: Agile methodology emphasizes the development of functional software features, valuing tangible results over comprehensive documentation. While documentation is important, the primary focus is on delivering working software.

Valuing interactions and individuals over processes and tools: Agile methodology places great importance on effective communication and collaboration among team members. Face-to-face interactions are encouraged, fostering self-organizing teams that leverage individual skills and expertise.

Continuously improving through reflection: Agile teams regularly reflect on their work, seeking opportunities for improvement. Through techniques such as retrospectives, they identify successful practices and areas for enhancement, making necessary changes to enhance their processes.

Agile methodology commonly employs frameworks such as

Scrum or Kanban to structure the development process. These frameworks provide specific guidelines for organizing work, defining roles and responsibilities, managing backlogs, and facilitating iterative development and feedback loops.

The goal of agile methodology is to deliver high-quality software in a flexible and efficient manner, with a focus on meeting customer expectations and adapting to changing requirements throughout the project lifecycle.

What is Scrum in Relation To Agile Methodology?
Scrum, a popular framework within the agile methodology, offers a structured approach to managing complex projects. It empowers teams to collaborate efficiently and achieve incremental delivery of high-quality software.

In Scrum, projects are divided into time-boxed iterations called "sprints," typically spanning two to four weeks. Within each sprint, a cross-functional team works collectively to deliver a potentially releasable product increment. Daily stand-up meetings are conducted to provide progress updates, address obstacles, and plan the day's tasks.

Scrum incorporates several key roles:

Product Owner: Represents the customer or stakeholders and defines project requirements. The Product Owner prioritizes the backlog and ensures the team focuses on delivering maximum value.

Scrum Master: Facilitates the Scrum process, helps the team adhere to Scrum principles, removes impediments, and ensures smooth operation. The Scrum Master is responsible for creating a productive and self-organizing environment.

Development Team: A self-organizing and cross-functional group responsible for delivering the product increment. The team members collaborate to design, develop, test, and deliver features according to the sprint goals.

Scrum also includes specific events or ceremonies to facilitate transparency, inspection, and adaptation:

Sprint Planning: The team plans the work for the upcoming sprint, selects items from the product backlog, and defines the sprint goal.

Daily Stand-ups: Short daily meetings where team members discuss progress, coordinate efforts, and identify any obstacles or issues.

Sprint Review: The team demonstrates the completed work to stakeholders, gathers feedback, and discusses potential adjustments to the product backlog.

Sprint Retrospective: A reflective session where the team assesses the previous sprint, identifies areas for improvement, and creates actionable steps for enhancing their process.

Scrum promotes iterative development, frequent inspection, and adaptation based on feedback. It provides a framework for teams to deliver value incrementally, collaborate efficiently, and respond effectively to changing requirements throughout the project.

Waterfall: The Waterfall model follows a sequential and linear approach to development, where each phase (requirements, design, development, testing, deployment) is completed before moving on to the next. In this model, games testers typically perform testing activities after the development phase, verifying the functionality and quality of the game.

What is the Waterfall model?
The waterfall model is a conventional and linear project management approach frequently employed by game development teams. It involves dividing the development process into sequential phases, where each phase relies on the completion of the previous one. Progress in the waterfall model

flows in a predetermined and structured manner, akin to a cascading waterfall.

Within game development teams, the typical sequential phases of the waterfall model include:

Requirements Gathering: The team collects and documents all project requirements, encompassing gameplay mechanics, visuals, audio, and other essential elements.

Design: Detailed design of the game's overall structure, mechanics, levels, and user interfaces is based on the gathered requirements. This phase involves creating wireframes, storyboards, and mockups.

Development: The game is coded and implemented according to the design specifications. Artists and audio professionals create necessary assets, while programmers write the code to bring the game to fruition.

Testing: Thorough testing is conducted after development to identify and resolve bugs and issues. This phase encompasses quality assurance testing, gameplay testing, and compatibility testing across different platforms.

Deployment: The final game is packaged, marketed, and distributed to the intended audience. This phase includes activities such as packaging the game, crafting marketing materials, and utilizing various channels for distribution.

The waterfall model operates in a sequential manner, mandating the completion of each phase before progressing to the next. Consequently, modifications or revisions made in one phase can pose difficulties and incur high costs when implementing them in subsequent stages. It necessitates a comprehensive understanding of requirements from the outset and offers limited flexibility to accommodate changes throughout the development process.

Although the waterfall model has enjoyed widespread usage in the past, it is gradually being supplanted by more adaptable and iterative approaches like agile methodologies, such as Scrum and Kanban. These agile methods provide enhanced flexibility, foster collaboration, and promote continuous improvement, making them better suited to the dynamic and evolving nature of game development projects.

Hybrid Models: Some game development teams may adopt hybrid models that combine elements of Agile and Waterfall approaches. For example, they may follow an Agile framework for iterative development while incorporating certain aspects of the Waterfall model for specific milestones or phases.

A hybrid model in game development combines elements of both waterfall and agile methodologies to leverage their respective strengths.

Here's an example of how a hybrid model could be implemented in a game development team:

Requirements and Design Phase (Waterfall): The project begins with a waterfall-like approach where the team gathers and documents the project requirements. This phase includes in-depth design planning, creating wireframes, and developing a comprehensive game design document (GDD). This phase aims to establish a clear vision and roadmap for the project.

Development and Testing Sprints (Agile): Once the initial design and planning are complete, the project transitions into an agile approach. The development work is divided into smaller, time-boxed sprints, typically lasting 1-4 weeks. During each sprint, a cross-functional team collaborates to develop, test, and deliver specific features or game mechanics. The team engages in daily stand-ups, sprint planning, and sprint reviews, ensuring frequent communication, feedback, and iteration.

Integration and System Testing (Waterfall): After completing the development and testing sprints, a waterfall-like approach is adopted to integrate all the developed features and conduct thorough system testing. This phase focuses on ensuring that all the components work together as intended, identifying and resolving any compatibility or integration issues.

Deployment and Post-Launch (Agile): Once the integration and system testing are successfully completed, the project shifts back to an agile approach. The focus turns towards finalizing the game, preparing it for deployment, and addressing any last-minute issues. The team continues to iterate and improve the game based on user feedback and post-launch analytics.

By combining waterfall and agile elements, this hybrid model allows for a structured approach during the initial planning and design phases while maintaining the flexibility, adaptability, and iterative nature of agile development during the implementation and post-launch stages.

The hybrid model aims to balance the need for thorough planning and documentation with the advantages of continuous collaboration, faster feedback cycles, and iterative development.

DevOps: DevOps practices emphasize collaboration and integration between development and operations teams. Games testers working in a DevOps environment are involved in the continuous testing and deployment of the game, ensuring quality throughout the development pipeline.

In game development, a DevOps model can be employed to enhance collaboration, streamline processes, and improve the overall efficiency of the development team. Here's an example of how a DevOps model can be utilized in a game development team:

Continuous Integration: The development team utilizes version control systems (e.g., Git) to manage source code. They regularly commit their code changes to a shared repository, ensuring that all changes are integrated and tested in a timely manner.

Automated Build and Deployment: The team employs build automation tools (e.g., Jenkins, TeamCity) to automate the process of building the game and creating deployable packages. This ensures consistency and efficiency when generating the game's executable files and assets for testing and deployment.

Continuous Testing: Automated testing frameworks, such as unit testing and integration testing, are implemented to validate the functionality and stability of the game throughout the development cycle. This enables quick identification and resolution of issues, reducing the likelihood of bugs reaching the final product.

Infrastructure as Code: The team leverage's infrastructure automation tools, like Ansible or Terraform, to manage and provision the necessary infrastructure resources, such as servers and cloud services. Infrastructure as Code enables consistent and reproducible setups for testing, staging, and production environments.

Continuous Monitoring: The game development team implements real-time monitoring tools to observe the game's performance, user behavior, and system metrics. This enables proactive identification and prompt resolution of performance issues, crashes, and anomalies.

Collaboration and Communication: To facilitate seamless communication and coordination among developers, testers, artists, and other team members, the team employs collaboration and communication tools like Slack or Microsoft Teams. This promotes effective collaboration and swift issue resolution within the team.

Continuous Delivery and Deployment: With the help of automated deployment pipelines, the team can efficiently deliver new features, updates, and bug fixes to players. Continuous integration and automated testing ensure the quality of the updates before they are deployed to production.

By adopting a DevOps model, the game development team can establish a collaborative and automated workflow, integrating development, testing, deployment, and monitoring into a seamless process. This approach allows for faster and more reliable delivery of high-quality games to players while enabling continuous improvement and iteration throughout the development lifecycle.

It's important to note that the choice of work practices can vary from one game development team or organization to another, and some may even create their own customized development models to suit their specific needs and constraints.

CHAPTER 8 - COMMON CHALLENGES IN VIDEO GAME TESTING

Video game testing can be a challenging and demanding process, with various obstacles that testers often face. One of the most common challenges is time constraints, as games are often developed under tight deadlines, leaving limited time for testing. Another challenge is the sheer complexity of modern games, which can be difficult to fully test due to their intricate systems, mechanics, and levels.

Additionally, the constantly evolving technology and hardware can create compatibility issues that need to be resolved. Communication and collaboration with the development team can also be a challenge, especially when it comes to reporting bugs and issues effectively. Finally, testers may also struggle with maintaining motivation and focus during the testing process, as it can be a repetitive and tedious task.

Tight deadlines and time constraints

As a video game tester, it is not uncommon to encounter tight deadlines and time constraints when testing a game. This can happen for various reasons, such as the need to meet a release date, catch up with unexpected delays during development, or respond to a sudden change in the market.

While tight deadlines and time constraints can be stressful, they can also provide an opportunity for testers to demonstrate their skills and expertise. Testers need to be able to prioritize their tasks effectively, focusing on the most critical areas of the game while also identifying and reporting bugs and issues in a timely manner.

To manage their workload effectively, testers need to be organized and have good time management skills. They must be able to estimate the time required for each task, allocate their time accordingly, and stay focused and motivated to meet their deadlines.

In addition, testers must be flexible and adaptable to changes in the development process, as unexpected issues can arise at any time, and the priorities may shift. They need to be able to adjust their testing plans and strategies quickly to accommodate these changes while still meeting their deadlines.

Finally, effective communication and collaboration with other team members, such as game designers and developers, can also help testers manage tight deadlines and time constraints. By working closely with the team, testers can get a better understanding of the game's development process and identify areas where they can make the most significant impact on the game's overall quality.

In conclusion, while tight deadlines and time constraints can be challenging for video game testers, they can also be an opportunity for them to showcase their skills and contribute to the game's success. By staying organized, flexible, and collaborative, testers can overcome these challenges and deliver high-quality results, even under pressure.

Here are some tips in order to help manage your time when working with tight time constraints on a project as a games tester:

Prioritize Testing: Focus on critical areas of the game that have a significant impact on gameplay, functionality, or user experience. Identify high-risk features or complex mechanics that require thorough testing and allocate your time accordingly.

Test in Iterations: Break down your testing into smaller, manageable iterations. Prioritize key features or specific aspects of the game in each iteration, allowing you to test and address issues incrementally within the available time.

Create Test Plans: Develop well-structured test plans that outline the testing scope, objectives, and specific test cases. Having a clear roadmap helps you stay organized, remain focused on essential areas, and ensure comprehensive coverage within the time constraints.

Test Coverage Strategies: Employ risk-based testing techniques to prioritize your testing efforts. Identify potential risks, vulnerabilities, or critical game elements and allocate more time and resources to thoroughly test them. This approach allows you to focus on areas that could have the most significant impact on the game's quality.

Automation and Tools: Leverage automation tools to streamline repetitive and time-consuming tasks. Automated testing can help with regression testing, performance testing, or specific gameplay scenarios, freeing up your time to focus on more exploratory and critical testing areas.

Efficient Bug Reporting: Optimize your bug reporting process by providing clear and concise bug reports. Include detailed steps to reproduce the issue, relevant screenshots or videos, and precise descriptions. This allows developers to understand and address the problems more efficiently, reducing back-and-forth communication and saving time.

Collaboration and Communication: Maintain open and effective communication with the development team. Regularly update them on your progress, challenges, and findings. Collaborate with developers to prioritize and address critical issues promptly, ensuring efficient use of time and resources.

Continuous Learning and Improvement: Embrace a growth mindset and continuously learn from each testing cycle. Identify areas where you can improve your testing approach, explore new techniques, and leverage feedback from the development team to enhance your testing efficiency in future iterations.

In the face of time limitations, it is crucial to uphold the quality of your testing endeavors. Prioritization, strategic planning, and proficient communication play pivotal roles in maximizing your testing efficiency within the given timeframe.

Complex game mechanics
and systems

Modern video games incorporate intricate and interdependent game mechanics and systems, posing considerable obstacles for game testers. These complexities span from elaborate combat systems in action games to sophisticated AI in role-playing games. Modifying or altering one element can potentially lead to unforeseen repercussions in other areas of the game.

Consequently, game testers must possess a comprehensive grasp of the game's mechanics and systems to ensure their proper functionality without adverse impacts on other game aspects.

Testers must be able to effectively communicate any issues or bugs they encounter to the development team, including any potential impact on the game's overall design and player experience. Therefore, testers must have a thorough understanding of the game's mechanics and systems, as well as strong communication skills, to ensure that the game is functioning as intended and delivering an enjoyable experience for players.

The need for constant adaptation and flexibility

Flexibility and adaptability are vital traits for video game testers. The dynamic nature of the game development process entails frequent additions and modifications to features, mechanics, and systems. These alterations can significantly influence the testing process, necessitating testers to swiftly adapt and modify their strategies to accommodate the changes effectively. Being able to readily adjust and embrace new testing approaches is crucial for success in this role.

One of the primary reasons for this need for adaptability is the iterative nature of game development. Games are typically developed in a series of iterations, with new features and mechanics being added to the game gradually. As a result, testers may be required to test different aspects of the game at different times, which can require them to adjust their testing plans accordingly.

Another reason for the need for flexibility is the fact that game development is often a collaborative process. Testers may be required to work closely with game designers, developers, and other stakeholders to ensure that the game meets the required standards. This collaboration may require testers to adjust their testing plans and strategies based on the feedback they receive from other team members.

Moreover, video game testing can often be unpredictable, with unexpected bugs and issues arising at any time during the development process. This means that testers need to be flexible in their approach, ready to adjust their testing plans and strategies as needed to ensure that all issues are identified and resolved.

In summary, being adaptable and flexible is essential for video game testers to be successful. It allows them to keep up with the fast-paced and ever-changing nature of game development and ensure that the game meets the required standards. This requires testers to have excellent communication and collaboration skills, the ability to adjust their testing plans and strategies quickly, and a willingness to learn and adapt as needed.

Dealing with player feedback and community management

As a video game tester, dealing with player feedback and community management is a crucial aspect of the job. Players often provide valuable insights into the game, including bugs, glitches, and other issues that need to be addressed. As a tester, it is important to not only take this feedback into account but also to communicate effectively with the development team to ensure that it is addressed in a timely manner.

Regularly engaging with the gaming community is a valuable approach to handle player feedback. This can be accomplished through multiple platforms, including social media, forums, and online communities. Actively participating in these channels and promptly addressing player feedback, inquiries, and concerns in a professional manner is crucial.

Aside from managing player feedback, game testers may also take on community management responsibilities, involving interactions with players and promoting the game. This can entail generating and sharing captivating content like screenshots, videos, and promotional materials to generate enthusiasm and curiosity surrounding the game.

Navigating player feedback and community management can present challenges. Diverse player opinions and expectations need to be balanced with the development team's goals and schedule. Testers must demonstrate adaptability, patience, and adept communication skills to address both player and team requirements effectively.

In the end, skilful management of player feedback and community engagement empowers testers to enhance the game's overall quality and foster positive reception within the gaming community.

Does AI pose a threat to games testers in the future and their jobs?

The role of AI in game development and testing is an evolving area that has the potential to impact the job landscape for game testers. While AI can automate certain aspects of testing, such as regression testing or performance testing, it is unlikely to completely replace the need for human game testers.

Game testing requires a deep understanding of game mechanics, player experience, and subjective aspects of gameplay. Human testers provide valuable insights and can identify issues that may not be detected by AI alone. They can also provide qualitative feedback, assess game balance, and evaluate the overall player experience. Additionally, human testers possess the ability to think creatively, adapt to unexpected situations, and make judgement calls that AI may struggle with.

AI technologies may augment game testing by automating repetitive tasks and providing additional data analysis capabilities. This can enable testers to focus more on complex and creative aspects of testing. AI can assist in identifying patterns, generating test cases, or improving efficiency. Rather than being a threat, AI has the potential to enhance the effectiveness and efficiency of game testing.

It is important for game testers to stay updated with emerging technologies and develop skills that complement AI, such as advanced analytical capabilities, understanding AI algorithms, and leveraging AI tools. By adapting and embracing AI as a tool, game testers can continue to contribute their expertise in ensuring high-quality games and a seamless player experience.

Example of Games Tester Working with AI on a test Scenario

Let's consider a scenario where a game tester is responsible for testing an open-world role-playing game. The tester is specifically focusing on the behaviour and interactions of non-player characters (NPCs) within the game world.

Traditionally, the tester would manually play through various scenarios, interacting with NPCs to observe their behaviour, dialogue, and responses. However, with the integration of AI into the testing process, the tester can leverage AI algorithms and techniques to augment their testing efforts.

In this scenario, the tester can use AI to simulate a large number of player interactions and scenarios with NPCs. By designing AI agents that mimic different player behaviors and objectives, the tester can observe and analyze how the NPCs respond and interact in various situations.

The AI agents can be programmed to explore different dialogues, quests, combat scenarios, and decision-making processes. The tester can then evaluate the NPCs' reactions, assess the accuracy of their responses, and identify any issues, inconsistencies, or unexpected behaviour.

By utilizing AI, the tester can scale up the testing process, simulate a diverse range of player behaviours, and identify potential edge cases that may have been challenging to cover through manual testing alone. This enables the tester to uncover bugs, improve NPC behaviour, and ensure a more immersive and engaging player experience.

While AI can improve the testing process, it is essential to acknowledge the indispensable role of human game testers. They are instrumental in shaping and refining AI agents, deciphering the outcomes, and making informed choices based on their deep knowledge of game mechanics and player expectations. Human testers bring their expertise and understanding to the table, ensuring that the testing process remains effective and aligned with the desired game experience.

CHAPTER 9 - THE FUTURE OF VIDEO GAME TESTING

With the continuous growth and evolution of the video game industry, the responsibilities of video game testers are also expanding. The emergence of cutting-edge technologies like virtual reality and augmented reality requires game testers to constantly adapt to fresh challenges and develop effective testing methods for these groundbreaking products. Furthermore, as an increasing number of games are developed as service-based offerings with regular updates and content releases, the tester's role in contributing to the ongoing success of the game becomes even more vital.

In conjunction with the rise of user-generated content and player communities, testers may also be required to provide support and engage with players in novel ways. This multifaceted approach to testing ensures that testers play an active role in shaping the gaming experience and fostering player satisfaction. All in all, the future of video game testing holds great promise, offering an exciting and dynamic landscape where testers push the boundaries of what can be achieved and help introduce innovative gaming experiences to players worldwide.

The impact of emerging technologies on game testing

As the gaming landscape undergoes continuous transformation, video game testing is taking on new dimensions, thanks to the emergence of advanced technologies. Among these ground breaking advancements, virtual and augmented reality have significantly influenced the industry.

With an increasing number of games embracing these technologies, game testers are faced with the crucial task of evolving their testing approaches to comprehensively assess the performance and functionality of games within these immersive environments.

Another emerging technology that is impacting game testing is the Internet of Things (IoT). As more games integrate IoT devices and technologies, such as smart home systems or wearable devices, game testers must ensure that the game's performance and functionality are not affected by the interaction with these devices. This means that game testers must have a solid understanding of the underlying technology and be able to test the game's compatibility with various devices and networks.

Artificial intelligence (AI) is also starting to make its presence felt in the world of game testing. AI-powered testing tools can help game testers to automate certain aspects of their testing processes, such as regression testing or performance testing, freeing up time for testers to focus on more complex tasks, such as exploratory testing. Additionally, AI can be used to analyze player feedback and behaviour, providing insights that can inform future game development and testing efforts.

Finally, cloud gaming is another emerging technology that is impacting game testing. As more games move to cloud-based platforms, game testers must ensure that the game's performance and functionality are not impacted by the cloud infrastructure. This means that game testers must have a solid understanding of cloud technologies and be able to test the game's compatibility with various cloud-based platforms.

In conclusion, emerging technologies are having a significant impact on game testing, and game testers must adapt their testing methodologies to keep up with these changes. By staying up-to-date with the latest technologies and tools, game testers can ensure that they are providing value to game development teams and helping to deliver high-quality gaming experiences to players.

The potential for AI and machine learning in game testing

As the video game industry expands, the intricacy of video games also deepens, consequently elevating the significance of game testing in the development process. In pursuit of enhancing efficiency and precision, the implementation of artificial intelligence (AI) and machine learning (ML) techniques is now being actively investigated to revolutionize game testing, enabling faster and more accurate evaluation methods.

One potential use of AI and ML in game testing is through the creation of automated testing tools that can simulate the actions of human players. These tools can perform a wide range of tasks, from identifying bugs and glitches to analyzing game performance and balancing. By automating these tasks, game testers can focus on more complex issues that require human intuition and creativity.

Another way AI and ML can be used in game testing is through the creation of predictive models that can anticipate and prevent issues before they occur. For example, by analysing player data and behaviour patterns, these models can predict potential bugs and glitches that may arise in a particular game mechanic or system. This can save game testers valuable time and resources by identifying and resolving issues before they become widespread.

The use of AI and ML in game testing is still in its early stages, and there are many challenges that need to be addressed. One of the biggest challenges is ensuring that these tools are able to adapt to the constantly changing landscape of video games. As game mechanics and systems become more complex and sophisticated, the tools used to test them must also evolve to keep pace.

Additionally, game testers will need to develop new skills and expertise in order to effectively leverage the capabilities of AI and ML in game testing. They will need to be able to work closely with data scientists and AI developers to create and fine-tune these tools, as well as analyze the data generated by them.

Notwithstanding these challenges, the potential advantages presented by AI and ML in game testing are immense. Their utilization holds the capability to substantially enhance the swiftness and precision of game testing while elevating the overall quality of video games. Consequently, it is highly probable that we will witness a growing adoption of these technologies in game testing in the forthcoming years.

The importance of continued innovation and improvement

The evolution of video games since their inception has paralleled the advancement of their testing process. As games grow in complexity and sophistication, the demand for testing that is both effective and efficient becomes paramount. Testing serves as an integral component of the game development process, ensuring that the final product adheres to quality standards and is free of bugs.

Given the ever-changing landscape of the video game industry, it is imperative for the testing process to stay abreast of technological advancements. In the following chapter, we will delve into the significance of continuous innovation and improvement in the realm of game testing.

As games become more complex, the testing process needs to adapt accordingly. With advancements in technology, testing tools and techniques have also improved, allowing testers to identify bugs and issues quickly and accurately. Automated testing tools and techniques have made testing more efficient and have reduced the time and effort required for testing. With AI and machine learning, the testing process can be taken to the next level, as it can help in identifying patterns and predicting potential bugs even before they occur.

The integration of novel technologies has revolutionized the scope of game testing, enabling a more comprehensive evaluation process. The utilization of virtual reality and augmented reality in testing facilitates the simulation of real-world scenarios, granting testers a deeper understanding of the player's game experience. Through this immersive testing approach, previously unidentified issues can be revealed, unearthing potential problems that might have gone unnoticed using conventional methods.

Another area that requires continued innovation and improvement is the process of reporting and documenting bugs. The use of bug tracking software has streamlined this process, allowing testers to report and track issues efficiently. However, with the increased complexity of games, the need for more advanced bug tracking tools and techniques has also increased. Tools that can provide more detailed and comprehensive reports can help developers identify and fix issues quickly, reducing the time required for testing.

Game testing is not just about identifying bugs; it's also about ensuring that the game provides an optimal experience to players. As such, the testing process should also focus on the overall quality of the game. This can include testing for factors such as game mechanics, graphics, sound, and user experience. Continued innovation in testing techniques and tools can help testers identify areas where improvements can be made, ultimately resulting in a better gaming experience for players.

Undoubtedly, the significance of ongoing innovation and improvement in game testing cannot be emphasized enough. As technology progresses at a rapid pace, the landscape of game development grows increasingly intricate, heightening the demand for effective testing methodologies. Embracing fresh testing techniques and tools becomes paramount for testers to remain at the forefront and guarantee that the final product attains the quality standards anticipated by players.

Therefore, game testers should continually seek out novel tools and techniques that can enhance their testing process, enabling them to contribute to the overall triumph of the game.

Closing Notes

To conclude, the realm of game testing awaits those ready to embrace boundless opportunities and unparalleled thrills. As the digital landscape continues its expansion, the role of a game tester emerges as a gateway to innovation, exploration, and the creation of extraordinary experiences.

By choosing a career in game testing, you open doors to a dynamic industry where you become an essential catalyst in transforming dreams into reality. Embrace the challenges, immerse yourself in the ever-evolving world of gaming, and witness the profound impact of your contributions first-hand.

Delight in the joy of uncovering hidden treasures, the exhilaration of pushing boundaries, and the deep satisfaction of ensuring exceptional quality for players around the globe. Embrace this captivating journey and embark on a thrilling path that allows you to play, test, and shape the future of gaming. The adventure awaits, and it all begins with your decision to become a game tester.

Get ready to make your mark on the vibrant tapestry of gaming's future!

Other Titles From The Author

Please check out some of my other titles on the topic of "Video Games" which is my favourite topic to write about:

"Level Up Your Gaming Career: A Comprehensive Guide To Become A Professional Gamer" released in April 2023.

Find these titles on Amazon as an E-book or they can be ordered as a paperback edition where available in your country.

UK Edition

US Edition

Thank you for reading this book.

www.ingramcontent.com/pod-product-compliance
Lightning Source LLC
LaVergne TN
LVHW051340050326
832903LV00031B/3660